EMOTIONS IN HISTORY – LOST AND FOUND

The Natalie Zemon Davis Annual Lecture Series
at Central European University, Budapest

EMOTIONS IN HISTORY–
LOST AND FOUND

Ute Frevert

CEU PRESS

Central European University Press

Budapest – New York

© 2011 by Ute Frevert

Published in 2011 by

Central European University Press
An imprint of the
Central European University Limited Company
Nádor utca 11, H-1051 Budapest, Hungary
Tel: +36-1-327-3138 or 327-3000
Fax: +36-1-327-3183
E-mail: ceupress@ceu.hu
Website: www.ceupress.com

400 West 59th Street, New York NY 10019, USA
Tel: +1-212-547-6932
Fax: +1-646-557-2416
E-mail: mgreenwald@sorosny.org

Cover design and layout by Péter Tóth

ISBN 978-615-5053-34-4
ISSN 1996-1197

Library of Congress Cataloging-in-Publication Data
Frevert, Ute.
Emotions in history : lost and found / Ute Frevert.
p. cm. -- (The Natalie Zemon Davis annual lecture series at Central
European University, Budapest)
Includes bibliographical references and index.
ISBN 978-6155053344 (pbk.)
1. Emotions--History. I. Title. II. Series.

BF531.F74 2011 152.4--dc23 2011027044
Printed in Hungary by
Akadémiai Nyomda, Martonvásár

Contents

and then – Chastity and family honour – Rape, sex, and national honour – The decline of honour, or its return?

Rage and insult – Power and self-control – Women's strength, women's weakness – Modernity and the natural order – Emotional topographies of gender – Sensibility – Romantic families, passionate politics – Intense emotions versus creative minds – Schools of emotions: the media – Self-help literature – More schooling: armies, peer groups, politics – Collective emotions and charismatic leadership – New emotional profiles and social change – Angry young men, angry young women – Winds of change

Empathy and compassion – Social emotions in 18th-century moral philosophy – Self-love and sympathy – Suffering and pity – Fraternité and the French Revolution – Human rights – Abolitionism and the change in sensibility – Sympathy, lexical – Schopenhauer's *Nächstenliebe* versus Nietzsche's *Fernsten-Liebe* – Compassion and its shortcomings – Counter-forces and blockades – Suffering, pity and the education of feelings – Modern dilemmas – Humanitarianism and its crises

List of illustrations

Preface and Acknowledgments

When Gábor Klaniczay invited me to give the Natalie Zemon Davis annual lecture in 2009, I had four reasons to immediately accept the invitation. First, I felt honoured to be connected to Natalie, whom I admire so much for many things that are mentioned in this book, and for more that are not. Second, I was thrilled to visit the Central European University and meet with its famous faculty and brilliant students. Third, I was excited at the prospect of seeing Budapest again, a city I had last visited in 1992, and experiencing first hand how it had changed. Fourth, the invitation forced me to clarify my ideas on a topic that has concerned me for some time: how to think about emotions in modern history, about their shape, influence, and dynamics.

My thanks go thus to Gábor and his colleagues, students and staff at CEU for giving me the opportunity to accomplish four tasks at once. They were generous hosts and offered me a warm and inspiring welcome. Their comments on the lectures were enormously helpful, and so was the criticism I received from my colleagues at the Max Planck Institute for Human Development in Berlin. The final manuscript owes a tremendous lot to our discussions and debates at the Institute's Centre for the History of Emotions. Uli Schreiterer gave my text a relentlessly critical reading and improved it in many ways. Kerstin Singer, Christina Becher and Kate Davison deserve my special gratitude for taking care of footnotes, illustrations and index as well as for polishing my rusty English.

The historical economy of emotions: Introduction

Brussels, 2010: Emotional politics and the politics of emotion

On September 16, 2010, Nicolas Sarkozy let off steam. Hitting back at the European Commissioner for Justice and Fundamental Rights who had sharply reprimanded the French government for the campaigns against illegal Roma camps, he did not care to hold back his anger. "I am the president of France and I cannot allow my country to be insulted," he declared at the Brussels summit. Viviane Reding's comments had been "deeply, deeply hurtful" not only to the French government, but also to his "fellow citizens." He considered them an outright "humiliation" and called them "outrageous," "disgusting" and "shameful."[1]

What had happened, and why did Monsieur le Président launch such a ferocious attack? Ms. Reding had obviously touched a raw nerve. It was already quite something that a commissioner had voiced severe criticism against a member state by accusing France of violating EU regulations and conducting a disgraceful policy. Furthermore, she had referred to the spectre of Vichy France and the wartime round-ups of Jews to draw a parallel with the present-day treatment of gypsies. This upset the French president. Over lunch with the Commission president José Manuel Barroso, he engaged in a fierce verbal argument. After lunch, Sarkozy addressed a news conference to continue the war of words. Interestingly, the vocabulary he used to rebuke the allegations drew from the lexicon of honour and shame: He spoke about humiliation and insult. He spoke about himself, his country and his fellow citizens having been humiliated and insulted, thus invoking highly charged notions of state and national honour. And he left no doubt as to the fact that the insult had been taken seriously. It was a "wound" that hurt deeply.

Emotions gained centre stage here. They were present in Sarkozy's words and voice, in his face and gestures. The French president was angry, and he made sure to show it. He lashed out passionately against his critics, although he himself maintained that he had been "the only person who remained calm and did not use excessive language" (which was contested by other witnesses). Both versions were perfectly in harmony with each other. Claiming that he had kept his temper and acted in a restrained rather than "excessive" manner was in accordance with the emotional style to which modern European and international politics adhere. At the same time, though, passions could not and should not be ruled out altogether. In exceptional, truly dramatic circumstances, they had to come to the fore. For Sarkozy, the situation was such that it demanded a straight and clear emotional statement. National honour was not an issue on which he was prepared to make compromises. And it was exactly this kind of honour that he felt had been offended by the "disgusting and shameful" comparison with Vichy and its anti-Semitic politics.

But there is more to this incident of passionate international politics. Emotions—anger and disgust—were not only part and parcel of the French president's reaction. Emotions were also involved in the cause that triggered the violent response: humiliation and insult. Insulting an individual or a group is synonymous with shaming them. It means taking away their honour and dignity, injuring or damaging their integrity. Humiliation deals a blow to someone's self-esteem; personal or collective pride is wounded by the feeling of being "put down," of being threatened in one's "personal integrity and wholeness."[2] Humiliation, as psychologists and social scientists argue, holds strong emotional power.

It goes directly against what individuals and groups consider their self-perception and how they want to be seen and treated by others. And it is highly subjective, as it depends on one's own views of what constitutes an insult even if these views are not shared by others.

The economy of emotions: How it works and why it matters

What does this story tell us about humiliation, anger and disgust and how does it relate to the topic of this book: emotions in history, lost and found? First, it points to the power of emotions in contemporary political life, both domestic and international. This tends to contradict the idea of politics that has been marketed throughout the modern era: politics is supposed to be a down-to-earth business, governed by dry procedures and conducted by unemotional, target-oriented personnel. Driven by interests and norms, it follows a rational logic, exemplified by the grey, colourless appearances of politicians and bureaucrats. Emotions, so it seems here, add colour to those appearances and performances, and, we may assume, to the underlying interests and norms as well.

Second, the story prompts us to ask how emotions work. What do words, facial expressions, voices and gestures disclose about emotions? Do they convey real emotions or faked ones? Are there any real emotions that might remain hidden in one's body or soul, and if so, how can we approach them? Or do we have to think of emotions as expressions of those inner feelings that bring them to the fore and communicate them to others? Could there be a difference between (inner) impression and (outer) expression? Is it conceivable that Nicolas Sarkozy did not feel angry or disgusted at all but rather wanted to make his audience believe that he felt this way? Did he display those emotions for other purposes? What can people achieve by "doing emotions"? And by which rules do they play? Can they invent their own rules and act accordingly, or do they more or less follow scripts that bear a more general meaning? Under which circumstances can they afford to disappoint expectations (in this case, for a politician to behave in a rational and restrained manner), and how can they make sure that affective language reaches its audience?

Third, the story raises questions as to how new this emotion talk and work is. To many observers, it seems as if we lived in a highly emotionalised age. Politicians have to show emotions, yet they are well advised to think twice about which emotions are appropriate for which occasion. When the Pope visited Jerusalem in

May 2009, his speech at Yad Vashem was criticised for lacking strong commitment and personal emotions. What he said about the Holocaust was seen as overly calculated, diplomatic and professional. The fact that he recommended empathy fell short of what the Israeli public deemed proper and desirable.[3] In a similar vein, election campaigns and inaugural speeches regularly play the emotions card by asking the citizens for their trust or evoking hope, by casting doubt on the opponent's trustworthiness and benevolent intentions.

Yet emotions are by no means restricted to the political realm. In order to sell products and services, the consumer economy coats them in emotionally charged images, sounds and words that promise happiness and well-being to buyers and users.[4] Sometimes, cars and cosmetics are bluntly called "Emotion" without any attempt to conceal their consumer lust-enhancing strategies. These are but the most recent examples of a much longer process that reaches back at least to the late nineteenth century, when economies in the US and Europe embarked on what has aptly been named *the making of the consumer*.[5] Even before that, commercial development and the culture of feelings reinforced each other. As early as the eighteenth century, sentimental fiction evoked goods as objects of emotional attachment that then became proliferated in economic life.[6] Emotions were thus rendered consumable and rose to public awareness and agency.

Just as "emotional capitalism" (Eva Illouz) was not invented in the twenty-first century but has a longer history, emotional politics is not a new arrival, either. Honour and shame are concepts that rest upon far more ancient notions of political power and legitimacy. Politicians driven (away) by passions are discussed time and again, and the era of mass politics presumably increased rather than diminished the appeal of emotions. It also served to foster emotional communication between citizens and their political representatives. Loyalty to the king was gradually replaced by trust in the government, which needed constant recalibration and fine-tuning. Distrust became a scourge for those political regimes that sought to invoke their citizens' cooperation by means of deliberation rather than coercion.

Those observations invite us to embark on an intellectual journey tracing the historical economy of emotions. The term originally stems from the Scottish philosopher Francis Hutcheson who, in 1728, wrote about the "oeconomy" of passions "which would constitute the most happy State of each Person, and promote the greatest Good in the whole."[7] Caring about such an economy was part and parcel of the project of modernity as it has developed in Europe since the eighteenth century. "Finding emotions" and exploring their relevance, importance and impact lends colour and taste to the project's texture that has preoccupied contemporaries and historians from its very beginning. But it also helps to retrieve aspects and dimensions of people's actions and mindsets that have been lost in translating the past to the present.

A case in point is, again, honour. Sociologists writing in the 1970s could rightfully claim that modernity denied the reality of honour and slander.[8] The cultural significance of honour that Max Weber was still acknowledging in the early twentieth century was on the wane. When German director Rainer Werner Fassbinder adapted his award-winning movie *Effi Briest* from Theodor Fontane's celebrated novel in 1974, the actress Hanna Schygulla confessed that she could not at all relate to the kind of honour Fontane wrote about in 1895. Eight decades later, she found it utterly strange and outmoded.[9]

Honour, thus, figures as a lost emotion, or, to be more precise, as a disposition whose emotional power has more or less vanished. Late-modern European societies and their intellectual interpreters have turned a deaf ear to honour's passionate demands that had resonated so compellingly in previous generations. The first chapter of this book explores how this change came about. Why and how did emotions get lost? Were they lost altogether, or did they live on under different names and labels? What happened to those social groups that had harboured and nurtured certain feelings and related practices for long periods of time and then chose to drop them? Can lost emotions resurface, as some present-day honour rituals, alongside Sarkozy's outburst in 2010, seem to suggest?

While the first chapter closely links emotions to social groups that feed and cultivate them before discarding them from their emotional economy, the second chapter tackles the question of how gender has structured emotional styles and regimes. Here, normative prescriptions come into play, meticulously seeking to align individual behaviour with highly gendered feeling and display rules. As with honour and shame, those rules became deeply embedded in the self-perception of women and men. A growing body of self-help literature as well as various other "schools of emotions" helped to vocalise rules and expectations and to translate them into personal attitudes and conduct. Gender, so the argument goes, served as the most conspicuous category that "naturalised" emotions while at the same time connecting them to distinct social practices and performances. This did not, however, leave emotions and related practices frozen in time. As much as men and women learned to negotiate and adapt gender relations to changing needs and desires, they also found new ways of coming to terms with what they were supposed to feel and how they should express those feelings.

The historical economy of emotions thus presents itself as dynamic and mobile, both enacting and reacting to cultural, social, economic and political challenges. It sees emotions and emotional styles fade away and get lost (like honour or acedia), but it also witnesses the emergence of new or newly framed emotions. Empathy and sympathy/compassion serve as great examples of emotions that are "found" and "invented" in the modern period. They are therefore addressed in the book's third chapter. Since the eighteenth century, empathy and sympathy have been regarded as civil society's primary emotional resources, connecting citizens and fine-tuning their mutual relations. They have fuelled humanitarian movements, from abolitionism to campaigns against cruelty, from giving shelter to escaping slaves to donating money for grief-stricken citizens in the present world. What stands behind this crucial reliance on empathy as a secular emotion? How did people learn it, and who did not? What prompted its success, and what prevented it from gaining full power? Are there limits to empathy, and how do we account for them in specific historical arrangements changing in the course of modernity?

The modern and the pre-modern

Considering the time frame of our intellectual journey into the historical economy of emotions, it could be argued that modernity did not actually start as late as the eighteenth century. For Natalie Zemon Davis, modernity began about two hundred years earlier, in the sixteenth century which, in her graduate training, she had come to see as the birthplace of "our modern ills and adventures: ferocious competition and capitalistic greed, but also hopes for change and the seeds of democracy."[10] At the same time, though, she was well aware that the sixteenth century (and the seventeenth to which she expanded her analysis later in her career) generated much more than "modernity" and that elements of the pre-modern coexist and interact with the modern in manifold ways. This holds true for the early modern period as much as for "high" and "late" modernity.

Focusing on the time period that starts in the mid-eighteenth century is not to deny, then, a vibrant pre-

or early-modern history of emotions.[11] Particularly in the field of art, the sixteenth and seventeenth centuries produced a wealth of emotion texts. In literature, theatre, painting, sculpture and music we encounter a surge in "affect poetics" that built on Aristotelian notions of various passions and connected them to aesthetic practices.[12] Affects and passions, in those days, were taken to be the prime movers of human actions, and consequently drew close scrutiny and constant monitoring. Regulating as well as expressing them through appropriate manners, looks, and words became a major concern of early modern polite society. Being sensible and behaving accordingly was a trait of seventeenth and early eighteenth-century aristocratic circles. It induced a vivid intellectual debate concentrating on questions of sincerity versus mask-wearing, of authenticity versus camouflage.[13]

Apart from being topics of contemporary discourse, emotions formed an integral part of pre-modern (as well as modern) religious, economic, social, and political culture. As early as 1919, Johan Huizinga, the eminent Dutch scholar of medieval history, wrote about the late Middle Ages as a period of exuberant passions. After the reformation, positive and negative extremes were balanced out; neither the grim hatred nor the risibility that had characterised the fourteenth and fifteenth centuries, lived on into the early modern era.[14] Twenty years later, sociologist Norbert Elias envisaged a similar scenario. Starting with absolutism, Europeans, he claimed, had learnt how to control their affects, instead of acting on an immediate impulse. The state monopoly of violence as it developed from the sixteenth century had triggered such learning processes as much as it depended upon them.[15]

Meanwhile, historians of medieval and early modern history have started to deal with those concepts of "rationalising" and "civilising" emotions as they have developed since the end of the Middle Ages. While some stress that Huizinga's image of uncontrolled, spontaneous emotions ruling over men's lives until the fifteenth century did not capture the strategic way in which emotions were used to convey notions of power and powerlessness, others have warned against applying an overly instrumentalised notion of emotions to the period.[16] Natalie Zemon Davis has not yet taken sides in this controversy. Her work, though, has a lot to tell about honour and shame, about feelings of fraternity and community in early modern *compagnonnage* systems, about mourning rituals and Protestant sensibilities when it came to the relief of the poor. From very early on, she looked at "rational interests" as much as on "façons de faire, façons de penser, façons de dire"—and, one might add, *façons de ressentir*.[17] But she did not turn the latter into a distinct research topic or into an analytical tool to open up new areas of historical investigation. This leaves us, her admirers and students, to venture into this new field and explore its potentials as well as its limits.[18]

By comparison to the pre-modern period, modernity as it is defined here takes a particularly strong and unique interest in emotions and what had formerly been called affect, passion, appetite or sentiment.[19] First and foremost, emotions have come to be considered as primary assets of a person's individuality and how she relates to others, i.e. her sociability. Arising in the body, they are felt and perceived by the person who inhabits that body. Rather than letting herself be overwhelmed by a sudden affect or consuming passion, the person is supposed to manage and control the manner in which she communicates her feelings through words, facial expressions, sounds and gestures.

How this could be done in a way conducive to the well-being of society was subject to a growing literature of moral philosophy and social conduct. The current craze about "emotional intelligence" gives only a recent example of a long tradition of advice books and coaching techniques aimed at enhancing a person's social capital and economic efficiency.[20] At the same time, the culture of "the therapeutic" which emerged in the twentieth century has reinforced introspection and emotional awareness as crucial means to individual psychic health and balance.[21] Again, this culture can easily be traced back to the eighteenth century which indulged in a great number of introspective measures. Reading novels, painting portraits and pastorals, and writing diaries and letters were promoted as methods of cultivating sensibility.[22]

Due to ongoing processes of literacy, urbanisation, industrialisation, and communication, modernity as an economic reality, as a political challenge, and as a large-scale social laboratory, engaged more and more people. It was not only thought about, but also lived and practised. The triumphal rise of science and its popularisation during the nineteenth century allowed for new theories and concepts to travel fast and reach an eager audience. Psychology, which gradually moved away from philosophy and metaphysical speculation made a powerful *entrée* into all sorts of domains: from industrial relations to commercial advertising, from individual therapy to political communication. In its wake, emotions gained attention and permeated public discourse as well as private conversations among lovers, friends, and family. Religious texts as well as literature, art, and music that had for a long time dominated the trade of modelling affects and reflecting on passions, were being increasingly complemented by scientific tracts and self-help manuals.

But what actually happened to emotions while they were analysed, measured, talked about, communicated, and managed? What happened to them during the period starting in the European Age of Sensibility and culminating in an era of high subjectivity at the end of the twentieth century? How did this affect their appraisal and appreciation? How did it shape the way in which emotions were gendered and class-bound? Were there emotions that got lost over the course of time? And how can historians find them?

Chapter 1

Losing emotions

Losing emotions in trauma

There are many ways in which emotions get lost. An individual can lose them as a direct result of a traumatic incident. Some of us might know someone who has undergone successful brain surgery. The tumour is gone, everybody is happy, except for the patient who can no longer experience happiness or sadness. Instead they start behaving in a strange and bewildering way. They have no empathy. They cannot relate to those who used to be very close to them before surgery. They do not even seem to care much about themselves.

Neuroscientists like Hanna Damasio and Antonio Damasio write about these cases. Their earliest and most prominent example is Phineas Gage, the railroad construction worker from New Hampshire, who suffered a horrible accident in 1848. A blast of powder carried an iron bar through his head damaging part of his brain tissue. Although Gage miraculously survived, he later suffered from all kinds of convulsions and died in 1860. The "melancholy affair" (as the Boston Post called it) brought him much fame, though, and he made frequent public appearances, proudly holding his iron. After his death, his skull was deposited (along with the bar) in the Harvard Medical School's museum, where it is still on display. Neurologists soon got interested in the case and tried to build all kinds of theories on it, connecting mental faculties to brain regions. Antonio Damasio, among others, used it to link frontal lobes and deeper brain centres that store emotional memories, to personal and social decision making. His assumptions, however, mainly rested on reports recording how Gage had mentally changed after the accident. Those reports have since been criticised as rather unreliable and hardly deserve the power of evidence attributed to them by later scientists.[23]

But there are more recent cases that allow for better-grounded hypotheses. Brain lesions and prefrontal damage are thought to impair a person's ability to process neural signals that form the basis of emotions. Cognitive skills might remain unharmed, and patients can carry on with their work, leading a seemingly normal life—except for issues that heavily depend on emotional investment. Perhaps not surprisingly, those issues turn out to be absolutely crucial and wide-ranging. Despite the patient's ability to solve logical problems and perceive their environment, they can no longer refer to their surroundings in an appropriate way. They prove unable to make sound decisions about their life, and they fail to properly display social emotions like embarrassment, sympathy, and guilt, which appear diminished or altogether absent. Since every decision, even the most rational one, implies emotions and is based, at least partly, on emotions, the absence of the latter, caused by brain damage, invariably has serious consequences.[24]

There are other ways in which a person might lose the ability to experience emotions. It does not have to be a brain lesion, a trauma in the medical sense of the Greek word. It can also be a psychological trauma: something people have experienced as a crucial event in their life, something that happened to them, that was done to them, with which they could not adequately cope. This kind of trauma might be associated with a blockage of feelings connected to the event and its memory. In this case, it is usually not the whole emotional system that is impaired and distorted. More often, it is particular emotions that are at stake here: emotions linked to psychic damage, such as pride and shame.[25]

Psychology and neuroscience have produced piles of evidence and a growing literature on these kinds of lost emotions. But how do historians approach the topic?

Losing emotions in psychology and historiography

They might first turn to psychologists for advice; after all, emotions have been on psychology's agenda ever since the discipline was founded. And indeed, the relevant literature starting with William James offers a wealth of definitions, explorations and classifications.[26] Still, emotions do not seem to be an easy topic. In 1984, there were many "questions about emotion" (to quote Paul Ekman's and Klaus Scherer's introduction to their volume), and a decade later, Ekman and Richard Davidson still asked "fundamental questions" on "the nature of emotion." Are there basic emotions? How do they function? How do we distinguish them from moods, temperament, and other related affective constructs? Are there universal emotions with a specific physiology? Can we control our emotions? Can they be experienced on an unconscious level? How do individuals differ in emotion-related activity? And what bears an impact on the subjective experience of emotion?[27]

The authors who attempted to answer those questions differed in almost every respect. They could not even agree on a common definition of emotion. Instead of interpreting such diversity as a lack of theoretical rigour and a symbol of disciplinary failure, we might take it as a sign of how complicated matters actually are. It did not help that scientific psychology, in its urge to cast off its philosophical shackles, dumped the traditional baggage of emotion words as they had developed over the centuries. Instead of distinguishing between passions and affects, between feelings and sentiments, between appetites and drives, the new psychological category of "emotion" came to encompass the wide range of mental states and bodily involvements of which humans are capable. It did not, however, integrate the in-built difference and ambiguity of those states, but rather forfeited much of their subtleties and incongruence.

A plethora of different emotional phenomena that had been linguistically addressed up until the nineteenth century thus got lost by grouping them under an all-encompassing new category. Psychology, especially in the wake of the 1990s turn to neuroscience, followed the scientific drive to explore basic dimensions and approximate qualities (positive/negative) of emotional states. In order to detect general principles and underlying mechanisms of human behaviour (survival/procreation, reward/punishment), the experimental setting has to reduce complexity and focus on a single or a few controlled variables.

Historians, in turn, are above all interested in the social and cultural complexity of emotions as well as in their historicity. They assume that the way in which people think and talk about emotions offers a clue as to how they experience and handle them. Ideas and concepts of what emotions are, and what they do, have clearly changed over time, and so have individual self-perceptions and emotional behaviour.

Historians also differ from present-day psychologists in the fact that they pay more attention to social emotions and how these play out in relational and collective settings. While most branches of psychology focus on the individual person who is, however, stripped of all individual traits and peculiarities, history looks at individuals in their capacity as members of social groups and institutions, as bearers of culture, as subjects of and to power. Here, the specifics matter, and they matter greatly. Situational and structural contexts are to be carefully examined and accounted for, since they offer particular incentives for individuals to act one way or another. Personal experiences as well as cultural memories and traditions are equally relevant in explaining someone's choices and decisions (or non-decisions).

Historians thus construct "thick" environments, rich with institutional complexity and personal detail. Consequently, they can hardly ever produce clear causal evidence. The reason why well-educated men and women in the late eighteenth century became infatuated with sentiments and sensibilities is not to be explained by, and attributed to, a single variable. Literacy was surely not enough, since one hundred years later many more people could read and write without being sentimentalists. The availability of books and the development of a specific reading culture do not offer convincing explanations, either. Rather, these phenomena themselves have to be explained: why did authors write sentimental novels and why did readers bother to care for the unhappy fate of Clarissa, Julie or Werther? Religion might be a case in point, and scholars have pointed to the affinities between Pietist faith and literary sentimentalism. But how do we account for the fact that Catholic Paris seemed to be as driven by the wave of *sensibilité* as Lutheran Frankfurt?

Every tentative answer to a causal question thus engenders new questions and answers, fuelling a never-ending debate about historical explanations and interpretations. Even when historians attempt to test a hypothesis by comparing similar cases with slightly different features, they have to struggle not to miss the complexity and peculiarity of those cases. The history of emotions principally poses the same difficulties and dangers as any other field or topic of historical research. Some scholars, though, consider it even more complicated and unfeasible to investigate. Emotions, so they suppose, are by definition fluid and unstable, they escape the historian's attention and remain hidden inside the human body. They seem to follow biological patterns that are impossible to be related to social or political events. As a part of human nature, they do not lend themselves to historicizing at all. They are, in one word, timeless and lost to historians.

Here, we encounter another dimension of losing and lost emotions. Academic historiography founded and crafted in the nineteenth century was not particularly eager to pick up on emotions as a topic of serious research. Although history books overflowed with passionate language and *telos*, authors hardly ever reflected on their own use of emotion words and images. They also refrained from systematically looking for emotions in their respective sources and analysing them in terms of functions, modes and causes. Only those who, by the end of the nineteenth century, had become interested in cultural history or were exploring the mechanisms of historical reasoning and understanding started to take an interest in "mental structural contexts," in "passions and pains" (Wilhelm Dilthey) or in the development of national feelings and sensibilities.[28]

Losing emotions in the civilising process

Those historians, though, remained as marginal as Norbert Elias who, as a young sociologist in exile, published his seminal studies on the civilising process in the late 1930s. For him (as much as for Huizinga), emotions had got lost on the way towards modernity. As he saw it, rationalising had progressed since the sixteenth century, gradually changing people's affective "apparatus." It led individuals to escape the "fog of personal affects and involvement," the "haze of collective longings and fears," and instead to be guided by experience and empirical evidence.[29]

But how true was this? Did empirical evidence not prove the exact opposite? Did Elias not write at a time when private and public emotions were exploding? Was he not aware of the fact that collective longings and fears were of paramount importance all over Continental Europe? Was he not personally affected by what Weimar intellectuals had already criticised as "boundless community morals"?[30] How could he make the claim that modernity and civilization went hand in hand when his own times testified to the opposite? At the very end of his book, we do catch a glimpse of Elias's personal perceptions and worries. "We scarcely realize how quickly what we call our 'reason,' this relatively farsighted and differentiated steering of our conduct, with its high degree of affect-control, would crumble or collapse if the anxiety-inducing tensions within and around us changed." Twenty years later, he acknowledged that civilisation could and had indeed broken down or moved backwards and was not necessarily to be viewed as a linear development.[31]

French historian Lucien Febvre had grasped this somewhat earlier. Writing in the late 1930s, at about the same time that Elias published his book, he urged his fellow historians to pay more attention to sensibilities and start a broad investigation of fundamental human emotions. Although he himself was an expert on the sixteenth century, he drew his inspiration mostly from what he observed in his own times: an over-abundance of what he called "primitive feelings." Among his contemporaries, he witnessed "revivals of the cult of blood, red blood," of the "cult of Mother Earth" and the healing sun, a quest for "cruelty at the expense of love." He found emotions dominating over reason and hailing "animal behaviour," and he warned that those emotions might soon turn the world into a "stinking pit of corpses."[32]

"Primitive feelings" which, according to Elias, should have been controlled and civilised through a centuries-long process of rationalising, had thus, in Febvre's testimony, returned to history. Once those feelings had finished their work of destruction, the historian settled in his Paris office and made notes for a lecture series on "Honneur et Patrie." He approached these concepts as "sentiments" that held a long history but were still alive "in our hearts" in the middle of the twentieth century. As a starting point and proof for his analysis, he recalled the dramatic situation after the French defeat in 1940. In its wake, France had seen two camps both pledging allegiance to honour and the fatherland. Young men went to war and fought one another on the same grounds. Both camps aligned themselves with the motto that crowned France's most prestigious order, the *Ordre National de la Légion d'Honneur*, founded in 1802. As much as Marshal Pétain and his Vichy regime appropriated its motto for their collaborative politics, General de Gaulle and his Free France movement used it as their slogan. Yet what honour meant and what kind of actions it entailed was clearly different.[33]

Febvre was highly interested in those differences and in the emotional power that the concept of honour (and fatherland) conveyed. Honour, he claimed, was a "mot-force" that appealed strongly to people, charged with history. In his lectures, he traced that history back to the Middle Ages, to the Song of Roland, and followed its path through the early modern period. As a personal attitude, as a "sensibilité" and as a force of action, honour had survived even in modern times, "toujours vivant [...] dans nos coeurs."[34]

But was this really the case? Or, more precisely, was it the same "sentiment," the same "sensibilité" that French philosophers of the seventeenth century had written about? As much as the honour that lived in the hearts of Pétain's and de Gaulle's followers differed from one another, we might assume that honour had also changed over time. Even if the word remained, its content and its references underwent serious alterations. What we, therefore, feel as honour is probably quite different from what our ancestors felt. Honour, in some respects, can be seen as an emotion that got lost over the course of history—though we still invoke it in our own times.

Losing emotions in words: acedia and melancholia

Before this strand is explored in more detail, let us look into the opposite case: an emotion whose name has indeed changed over time. What does that tell us about the emotion proper? Does the change of words mean that the emotion has changed as well? Or is there perhaps no direct link between the word and what it signifies? The case in point here is *acedia*, which in ancient Greece meant a kind of listlessness, of not caring or not being concerned with one's position or condition in the world.[35] An English translation would be sloth, Germans call it Trägheit. In Antiquity and during the Middle Ages, acedia was particularly noted as a problem amongst monks and other ascetics who led a solitary life. Thomas Aquinas writing in the thirteenth century defined it as "the sorrow of the world" contrasting it to "spiritual joy." It was conceived as a demon that could strike at any time and infuse tedium or boredom. Closely related to tedium was a general laziness or refusal to work, a temptation that frequently befell the monastic at rest. Another characteristic of acedia was the lack of the desire to read or pray.[36]

To people of the twenty-first century, this feeling might seem quite familiar. They, too, feel lazy at times, they procrastinate and do not like to carry out the tasks required by their job. But is this *acedia*? Is this the highly charged state of mind and feeling that the ancients described so lucidly? This is more than doubtful. First, the symptoms seem to differ. Premodern sources talk about corporeal signs that range from mere sleepiness to general sickness or debility, alongside a number of more specific ailments: fever, pain in the limbs and weakness in the knees. Second, and even more important, the interpretation of those signs was very peculiar and does not fit into today's mental map. For the ancients, the bodily signs did not just signal a certain state of mind. Instead, they demonstrated the presence of a demon, some external influence that invaded the body and transformed it for the worse. The body was therefore thought to be utterly permeable and malleable. What mattered most was that the soul had the strength and willpower to cast off those influences and protect the body from falling ill. Somatic signs of the demon's activities thus meant, in the last instance, that the spirit was too weak to fight and gave way to sin and vice. Suffering from *acedia* then ultimately placed guilt on the individual who suffered: his dedication to God, his veneration of God, was simply not strong enough and had to be rebuilt at all costs.

Such an interpretation is not what most Europeans believe in at present. They would probably turn to stress theory and assume their laziness reflected a lack of energy. This might have multiple causes: too much or too little work, lack of motivation, general exhaustion, burn-out or bore-out syndromes. They would not be likely, however, to be concerned with personal guilt, and they would definitely not consider themselves deadly sinners if they did not fulfil their duties.

But what about the modern age inventing new names for similar states of distress, like melancholy? The word *melancholia* that gained prominence in the early modern period derives from the ancient medical theory of the four humours associated with bodily fluids. Melancholia was thought to be caused by an excess of black bile, and was accompanied by sadness, low levels of enthusiasm and no inclination to become actively involved. The German name is *Schwermut*, meaning that the *Gemüt*, which might vaguely be translated as the soul, carries a heavy load. *Melancholia* could express itself both through bodily and psychic symptoms, but it was different from *acedia* as there was no laziness, no *Trägheit* involved. Furthermore it was viewed as an internal state, not caused by any external demon, and it was not judged as unequivocally bad. There is a famous engraving by Albrecht Dürer entitled Melencolia I, dating from 1514. Here, the female allegory is portrayed in a pensive mood, perhaps wait-

Fig 1.
Albrecht Dürer, *Melencolia I* (engraving, 1514).

ing for inspiration. The original is far lighter than its reproductions, and so are the woman's face, and, in particular, her eyes.[37] In this way we might see her

34

not necessarily in a state of depression, knocked down by anxiety, weakness and inertia, but in a state of expectation that in the sixteenth century was associated with creativity and ingenuity.[38]

Talking about depression takes us to the twentieth century. The term entered the psychological lexicon in 1905, and since then it has seen a breathtaking career. It is considered a mental illness that affects, at least in Western countries, up to one in five people at some point in their lifetime. Its symptoms include loss of interest or pleasure, feelings of sadness, or little to no emotion, feelings of fatigue, guilt, helplessness, anxiety, and fear, often for little or no reason. The direct cause is attributed to neurobiological disorders, the level of neurotransmitters being either too high or too low.[39]

Up to now, we have identified three states of mind, soul and body that at first glance seem to share certain symptoms. This might lead us to think that they are basically the same. But are they? The resemblance ends when we take into account that they are explained, interpreted and valued quite differently. This in turn makes an impact on how *acedia*, *melancholia* and depression are framed and felt by those who suffer from them. The fact that acedia is considered a mortal sin, an affront to both God and the religious community, is bound to influence the way that a monk or a nun of the thirteenth century experienced it. A seventeenth or eighteenth-century writer who feels melancholy will have a completely different self-perception, which shapes his way of being affected by *Schwermut*; and a twentieth-century person on anti-depressants thinks differently again about what is wrong with their bodily chemistry. Knowing that so many others are going through similar experiences might put one's own ailment into a different perspective. Thinking of neurotransmitters and synapses allows for an approach that is different to pondering over temperaments and fluids, black bile, demons and sinning against God and the community.

So the central argument is the following: Even if there are signs of *acedia*, *melancholia* and depression that resemble each other, the labelling, framing and contextualising of those signs are vastly different. Relating the symptoms to diverse systems of reference (magic, religion, arts and sciences, neurobiology) affects the value attributed to them. This in turn affects the appraisal and experience of those states. Seen from this perspective, *acedia* and *melancholia* are indeed "lost emotions," lost in translation to a new emotional state called *depression*.

Losing the mot-force: *honour*

A similar point might be made regarding honour. In contemporary Western emotional lexicons, honour does not feature prominently. Febvre's contention in 1945-46 that honour was alive and well soon found itself challenged. The political culture of post-war Western Europe was decidedly less pathos-driven than it had been during the Second Thirty Years War that had raged between 1919 and 1945. Even though the rift between Communist and non-Communist countries gave rise to a high degree of political anxiety and insecurity, those worries were framed in a different language. The old *mots-force* lost their ideological substance, existential power and emotional appeal, both in private and in public life. People seemed to be exhausted by their overuse and kept their distance.

This held true particularly for Germany which had seen an upsurge of those words during the preceding years. Honour and fidelity had ranked highly on the list of values that the National Socialist regime had tried to enshrine in social and political institutions. "Alourdis d'histoire," as Febvre observed for the French case, these emotions had been marketed as genuine "racial" German faculties. At the same time, they had been charged with great expectations and duties. Something as exclusive and eminent as German honour had to be safeguarded by all means. In 1935, the parliament passed a law "to protect German blood and German honour." It forbade Jews (identified as non-German) to marry Germans (identified as non-Jewish), and it harshly sanctioned any sexual encounters between them. In addition, it barred Jews from employing German maids younger than 45, and it put a ban on them wearing or hoisting German colours. Honour here was closely associated with the "purity of blood" and with national symbols. A year later, the *Parteitag der Ehre* (rally of honour) met in Nuremberg to celebrate the restitution of German honour. That honour had, so the argument went, been seriously harmed by the Versailles treaty. The Allied Powers had not only held Germany responsible for World War I; they had also curtailed her sovereignty by suspending military conscription and demilitarising the Rhineland. In 1935, the National Socialists reintroduced conscription, and in 1936, they stationed *Wehrmacht* troops in the region. Honour (bound to sovereignty) had thus been restored.

Neither sovereignty nor sexuality featured in those concepts of honour that survived the Nazi period and lived on in East and West Germany. The honours that the respective governments bestowed on their citizens had nothing to do with the purity of blood. Instead, the state acknowledged and rewarded special merits and services for the community. Medals, orders, and decorations were and are conferred in order to "honour" exceptional deeds and virtues.[40] In a similar vein, people appreciate honorary appointments, degrees and titles given to them by institutions like universities, associations, or parliaments. Honorary citizenship is conferred to those who have been of particular esteem and importance to a state or city, as when Winston Churchill was bestowed with the US citizenship in 1963 by an act of the Congress. In Germany, voluntary work is considered an "honorary office" (i.e. it is done *pro bono*). To give one's "word of honour" means pledging one's good faith. It is still in use, especially among children and adolescents who want to make sure that they are not being deceived. The law, too, accounts for honour and, under certain, well-defined circumstances, considers insults as an honour offense.[41] Honour has thus not completely vanished from today's mental map. In contrast to *acedia*, the term is still known and used.

But what about its meaning? Do we attribute the same valence, the same emotional weight and urgency to notions of honour as our grandparents or great-grandparents did? Do we attach them to identical issues and practices? Do we gender them in similar ways as in the nineteenth century? Do we distinguish between lower or upper-class honour? Do we consider honour as an ethnically neutral phenomenon, or do we associate it with certain groups and cultures more than with others? In short, is the type of honour that still seems roughly familiar to contemporaries, equivalent or comparable to those types that have traditionally been defined as belonging to earlier periods of European history? Or, for that matter, to non-Western cultures cherishing a sense of honour and honour practices which seem to have been lost in mainstream Western societies?[42]

Honour as an emotional disposition: Internal/external

Some people might even doubt whether honour counts as an emotion at all. It surely does not figure on the shortlist of basic emotions that psychologists have put together. It is also missing from most of the longer lists. But this should not concern us too much. Experimental psychology is a modern Western science, and deals with modern Western subjects who usually do not seem to care much about honour and are oblivious to its emotional thrust. Only rarely do psychologists extend their scope of questions to encompass experiences that are not shared by middle-class Western university students.[43]

If we asked anthropologists or social scientists about the emotional power of honour, we would encounter a different response. The French sociologist Pierre Bourdieu, who started his career studying honour cultures in Algeria, described honour as a powerful *habitus*, as a system of emotional "dispositions" that in turn produces and structures social practices.[44] Lucien Febvre called it a sentiment or a sensibility that lived in our hearts.[45] Nearly two centuries earlier, an anonymous author likewise found honour "rooted in the heart."[46] The heart, in those days, was considered to be the organ from which emotions sprang. Honour is "physiologically felt," wrote another expert in 1904. It obviously manifested itself alongside bodily symptoms which, according to contemporary psychologist William James, were thought to be emotion proper.[47]

Learned men who published articles about affect and passion for the encyclopaedias of the eighteenth and nineteenth centuries never hesitated to name honour and its derivatives (*Ehrgeiz, Ehrtrieb, Ehrliebe*) among the most noteworthy emotions. Montesquieu, writing in 1748, defined honour to be the "spring" of monarchical government. Instead of virtue that inspired republics, monarchies were based on "pre-eminences and ranks" and thus on honour "that is the prejudice of every person and rank."[48] Even if every person and rank claimed honour in early modern societies, there were vast differences between social classes or estates, between men and women, and between different religious and ethnic groups. All of them developed their own codes of honourable conduct which had to be strictly observed by group members. Losing one's honour due to violating those codes and/or being banished from the group was tantamount to suffering social death.[49]

The social and cultural importance of honour was not lost on modern societies, either. Sociologists like Max Weber or Georg Simmel around 1900 testified to its ongoing presence. Honour still played a vital role in informing and regulating people's behaviour. Sociologically speaking, it served as the "glue" that bound a social group together and fostered cohesion among its members. While law, as Simmel noticed, stabilised society at large, and morals guided individual behaviour, honour was the safeguard of intermediate social groups or circles. Its special service was seen in its ability to push "external purposes" through "internal means." Each group member was taught to embrace honour as his or her most individual concern. Social duties were thus translated into "individual salvation" and self-interest. As such, honour functioned as a perfect hybrid: although it was integral to a social group and its particular rules of conduct, it was appropriated by individuals as a "purely personal" thing. It was regarded as a deeply emotional matter linked to people's self-concept in two ways: it directly related to their claims to personal integrity and their aspirations to social recognition and reputation.[50]

How this worked can be neatly studied in the case of nineteenth-century upper and middle-class men. In countries like Germany, Austria-Hungary and parts of Switzerland, but also in France, Spain, Italy and Russia, they were exposed to an honour regime with massive institutional and personal ramifications. In terms of social institutions, membership in students' associations as well as military recruitment introduced them to strict codes and practices of honour. As students and officers, they learnt not only to take their honour very seriously but also to defend it by all means. They were taught to watch out for possible insults and not to let them go unanswered. Being a member of a student fraternity required extreme sensitivity about honour. Whoever behaved in a dishonourable fashion lost his legitimate place in the group. Still worse was the group member who allowed himself to be treated dishonourably by someone else, within or outside the group. This behaviour was considered utterly despicable, since it displayed an eminent lack of courage and character. In this vein, being called a coward, or a cheater, or getting physically attacked commanded strong counter-action. Right or wrong, what was perceived as offending one's honour had to be redressed immediately and with full force.

Similar rules applied to the army. Officers, noble or middle-class, were trained to safeguard their honour as a professional asset of crucial importance. As they were acting as members and on behalf of a venerable institution, they had to behave in a way that kept the institution's honour unharmed. Whoever dared to insult it (by not paying adequate respect, or by openly trespassing against its principles) was punished accordingly. This held true for the officers' own conduct, as much as for civilians who disregarded the special reputation that the army claimed for itself and its members. Anyone offending an officer also offended the institution, and vice versa. Officers were thus known as a particularly honour-conscious group of men, who definitely took honour "to heart" and were eager to defend it whenever and wherever possible and necessary. They considered themselves true men of honour who were imbued with *Ehrliebe*, love of honour of the highest kind. And they were, time and again, reminded of what honour required them to do (and not to do) by their commander-in-chief. In 1874, Wilhelm I, Prussian King and German Emperor, let everybody know that he would not tolerate any officer offending the honour of a comrade, or any officer who failed to guard his own honour.[51]

How could honour be offended? Actions that were deemed irreconcilable with an officer's honour were those that showed a lack of determination or discretion, debts, unsuitable social company, gambling or alcohol abuse. Apart from these manifest transgressions, officers might feel hurt by a dismissive remark, a wry look, by not being greeted or invited to a dinner party. Verbal insults were topped by physical assaults: a punch, a slap in the face or a stroke with the sword. If worst came to worst, an officer found his "domestic" or "family honour" violated, meaning that a comrade had seduced his daughter or wife.[52]

In the light of such dishonourable acts, honour can thus be positively described as an emotional disposition focusing on a person's moral and physical integrity. Violating this integrity brought disgrace on the person who had been offended. Above all, it meant lowering and shaming him in front of an audience of

45

peers. Those peers were concerned about the offence and demanded a vigorous reaction. A man who failed to react in an appropriate way, who shied away from calling the offender to account, was judged a coward. It was implied that he deserved the insult by not being emotionally involved and eager to protect his honour. This was the case with a Bavarian officer in the 1840s. A pharmacist had insulted him as a "scoundrel," a slander for which the offender was taken to court and given a prison sentence. This, however, did not satisfy the officer who found himself cornered by his comrades. To retain their respect, he planned to take stronger personal action.[53] A similar case became known and immortalised in literature: in Arthur Schnitzler's novel "Lieutenant Gustl" from 1900, an Austrian officer feels publicly humiliated by a man who is of inferior social status. As he fails to respond appropriately (i.e. strike down the other with his sword), he decides to commit suicide. This to him seems the only way to wipe off the stain that the other had left on his honour's clean slate.

As Simmel observed so lucidly, honour here worked both ways. On the one hand, it was deeply embedded in professional and institutional codes. The officer corps demanded a specific conduct and imposed negative sanctions on members who failed to meet those demands. Contemporary critics thus attacked the honour code as compulsion and coercion. On the other hand, the code was carefully and smoothly translated into individual mindsets and demeanour. To safeguard one's honour was considered and felt to be a strictly personal matter, profoundly and intimately in one's own interest.

As a personal issue, it called for a holistic approach. It was not enough to take the offender to court and have him convicted for slander and libel. Although the law had made relevant provisions, men were rarely inclined to accept them. In Germany, the Anglo-Saxon logic of financial compensation was met with harsh criticism. Even Lujo Brentano, a liberal social reformer and admirer of British institutions, disapproved and found it incommensurate with the immaterial character of personal honour.[54] Germans generally privileged the idea of the "whole man," of the autonomous personality who masterfully managed to integrate moral and material concerns. Heart and brain, emotion and reason had to act in unison. As much as an insult affected the "whole man" in his "right to exist," that man had to take personal responsibility for asserting his right. Since honour was seen as one and indivisible, it demanded full action to preserve one's "moral and emotional integrity."[55] Even Karl Marx, a reliable critic of bourgeois morality, felt sympathetic towards men who refused to bargain over their "individuality." In certain situations, he argued, they could not help but take recourse to "feudal forms" in order to prove it.[56]

Honour practices: The duel

What did Marx have in mind? What kind of "feudal forms" was he referring to? His remarks came in response to a letter by Ferdinand Lassalle in 1858. Lassalle, a German-Jewish writer and socialist activist, had been called out to a duel by a civil servant, but since he opposed duelling, he had refused. Yet, as he confessed to a close friend, it had been hard for him to "suppress the desire of my blood in favour of my principles." As a member of a student fraternity, he had learnt to value honour highly and observe the relevant comment. His first reaction to the challenge had thus been a passionate one: he had felt "an extremely vigorous drive" to accept it under even harsher conditions. When he saw reason and rejected the challenge, he nonetheless feared for his reputation. The prospect of people interpreting his behaviour as an act of cowardice tormented him. It came close to "annihilation" and hurt his "vanity."[57] Six years later, he withstood annihilation and let vanity, individuality and honour reign. By then the founder and president of the first social-democratic party in Germany, he sent a challenge to the man who had refused to let him marry his daughter. The duel took place on August 28, 1864. Lassalle was shot and died three days later, aged 39.[58]

Lassalle was one of many "men of honour" who populated Europe during the nineteenth and early twentieth century. Duelling, which had originated in early modern Spain, proved very much alive and part of the "bourgeois experience" as Peter Gay aptly called it.[59] Even though Marx referred to it as a feudal form, it had undergone a drastic change of substance and appearance. Advice literature and handbooks had worked to transform it into a highly regulated and controlled encounter. It was still regarded as an act of passion, but the ritual itself did not match this concept. Duellists were supposed to behave calmly and in a restrained manner. They were not allowed to curse or insult each other but had to keep their distance. Seconds ensured obedience to the rules and fair play.

Among the gentlemen who took to duelling figured eminent politicians, professors, doctors, lawyers, and entrepreneurs. Wilhelm von Humboldt was one of them, a high-ranking civil servant and founder of Berlin's first university. In 1815 he was Prussia's envoy to Vienna where European politicians decided on the future of Europe after the defeat of Napoleon and his revolutionary armies. Another member of the Prussian delegation was Hermann von Boyen, Prussian minister of war. On one occasion, Humboldt urged Boyen to leave a meeting with the Austrian chancellor, Duke Metternich. He did not mean to offend Boyen, but the latter obviously felt that way. Even after Humboldt apologized, Boyen would not calm down and only relented when Humboldt offered him a duel. They met, they took aim, they shot, yet they both chose not to hit the other. Right after the duel, they talked in great harmony and were at peace with one another—which, as Humboldt confessed to his wife, would never have happened without the duel.[60]

Sigmund Freud, the founder of psychoanalysis, was equally sensitive about honour. In 1885, as a young doctor at the Viennese General Hospital, he told his fiancée about a duel that his colleague and friend Carl Koller had with another colleague. The latter, after a minor dispute, had insulted Koller as a Saujud, an anti-Semitic slur for which Koller had retaliated with a slap in the face. Both the verbal and the manual slip were considered serious slanders and should have resulted in a duel. Freud was obviously happy about Koller's response and sent him a bottle of wine so that he could gain strength before the fight. He found it important to protect the honour of Jewish men and citizens, and was full of pride and joy that Koller had acted in a manly and courageous way.[61]

A last case in point—of which there are many more—is Max Weber. The famous sociologist, who considered himself a proud member of the middle classes, repeatedly talked and wrote about honour as a pre-modern pretension. At the same time, he was extremely thin-skinned when it came to his personal honour. He never hesitated to call out colleagues who, as he saw it, had insulted him or his wife. Although Marianne Weber was an outspoken feminist, she obviously did not mind him defending hers and his honour. Later on, she reported that her husband harboured very "irascible" and passionate feelings of honour and fought hard to sustain them.[62]

Those feelings were by no means restricted to German or Austrian men. In 1804, US Vice President Aaron Burr challenged Federalist Alexander Hamilton to a duel in which the latter was killed. Three years earlier, Hamilton's son Philip had died at the same duelling site.[63] In 1829, the Duke of Wellington, as British Prime Minister, called upon the Earl of Winchilsea "to give me that satisfaction for your conduct which a gentleman never refuses to give." The Earl responded immediately and found it "of course impossible for me to decline" the request. The two gentle-men met at Battersea Park in London. The Duke shot first, but apparently did not aim at his opponent. The latter then fired in the air. After having given "the usual satisfaction," the Earl publicly declared his re-gret for having accused the Duke of "disgraceful and criminal motives."[64] In 1891, the British Vice Consul in Paris acted as a second to a duel causing the House of Commons to passionately debate the case. At that time, the British had by and large abandoned the cus-tom of duelling at home.[65] However, it survived in the Continent, above all in France where the duel was cherished by monarchists, republicans, conservatives and socialists alike.

But why, we may ask, did men duel? Why did they choose to carry their honour, as Rousseau framed it, on the tip of their sword? Why did they risk their lives in order to save their honour? Contemporaries called the idea of duelling "a true paradox of self-love": through acting out of self-love, duellists destroyed its foundation—their physical existence.[66] Such behav-iour poses an unresolved puzzle for any evolutionary biologist or rational choice economist. Men of hon-our were not in the least driven by material interest or gain. Rather, they went for something immaterial, spiritual and emotional.[67] They acted in an extremely self-centred and self-possessed way when taking every offence to heart and listening exclusively to their own sense of honour and righteousness. They brushed off all concerns for their own life and that of others, including the well-being of family members. Whenever they felt insulted, men would call each other out, and fight to the last drop of blood in order to save their honour. Why? What was so compelling and attractive about the duel?

The emotional power of duelling

In order to find out, we have to listen to those who fought and defended it. There were others, obviously, who abstained from the custom and condemned it as stupid, dangerous and irrational. Criticism had been around as long as the practice existed. All pros and cons had already been discussed at the beginning of the nineteenth century. A hundred years later, critics were even more outspoken. They dominated parliamentary debates and newspaper reports, they hijacked literature and religious sermons. They organised rallies and founded associations like the anti-duelling league that were active in many European countries. Yet, despite their efforts, duelling persisted as a social practice.

In part, this can be attributed to the ongoing power of supportive institutions: student fraternities and the army. Still, it would be misleading to think of duelling mainly as a ritual forced upon their members. On the contrary, duellists prided themselves on holding motives of their own. Even Marx, who strongly disapproved of duelling as a social convention, tolerated it as an expression of individuality. The same held true for Max Weber, who openly defended the duel in certain situations, but denounced those who were blindly following the custom and using it for minor purposes.[68] Weber's colleague Adolf Wagner, who was challenged by a well-known industrialist in 1895, eloquently described his ambivalence on the matter. On the one hand, duelling was forbidden by law which, as a civil servant, Wagner had a strong commitment to obey. On the other hand, he felt equally committed to the "passions" and "opinions" of his academic and middle-class circles. The rift, he knew, could not be healed. Yet it could be narrowed by restricting the duel to truly serious cases of slander. In those cases (like physical assaults, or attacks on the "family honour"), duels still seemed the only acceptable answer. To stress their exceptional status, though, they were supposed to be fought under extremely hard circumstances: "Whoever calls out or accepts a duel has to be forced to face an emergency"—meaning that they might lose their lives.[69]

Death figured prominently on men's mental map. Indeed, duellists wrote farewell letters to their loved ones or drew up their last will in the night before they met their opponent. They were well aware that they faced death at dawn. Even if the offence had been trivial, thus softening the rules (in terms of distance, number and order of shots) and reducing the risk, one could never be sure about the outcome. One could also never be sure of one's own emotions, let alone about those of the opponent. When Humboldt confronted Boyen in 1815, he did not know, as he later confessed to his wife, if Boyen was really determined to shoot him. He knew Boyen had been furious about the offence and held "serious ideas" about the duel. At the duelling site, he saw him taking aim with care and precision— until, when Boyen finally pulled the trigger, he turned the pistol into a slightly different direction. Humboldt was left with "strange and peculiar" feelings.[70]

In 1852, Otto von Bismarck had a similar experience after he had called out the liberal politician Georg von Vincke. He was doubtful whether he should shoot at Vincke at all. Eventually, he did, albeit "without rage," as he wrote to his mother-in-law. And he told her, somewhat surprised, about his "feeling of discontent" after he had noticed that Vincke had not been hit. He could not join in the chorus cheerfully greeting the bloodless outcome, but would have preferred to continue the fight. That the exchange of shots had been limited to one caused him "displeasure" and "annoyance." Only somewhat later, when his "blood had cooled down," he changed his mind and felt "very grateful" considering the undramatic result.[71]

Facing death and facing one's own lust to kill (or maim) generated noteworthy emotions. They took men by surprise and overwhelmed them to such an extent that they felt the urge to share them with family and close friends. As a general rule, duels followed a highly ambiguous emotional script. On the one hand, they were seen as terminating a conflict that had aroused strong, sometimes even violent emotions. Men felt shamed and humiliated by an insult which had stirred their anger and rage. Yet, instead of retaliating in the same manner or even worse, they called the other person out. Anger and rage were transferred into regulated action. It involved third parties who served as seconds and tried to mediate. The time that elapsed between the insult and the duel was another method to pacify hearts and minds. On the site, then, duellists were supposed to display a restrained and controlled demeanour. Even if their blood was still boiling, they were not supposed to show it. All precautions taken were meant to deflate the situation and allow for detached, polite and "civilised" behaviour. Initial rage was thus transformed into noble restraint and fair play.

On the other hand, the duel itself was not without emotion, but rather confronted the individual with feelings that appeared strange and that he did not expect. Humboldt alluded to fear and anxiety, Bismarck wrote about his desire to see blood. Others evoked the serenity of the moment and a sense of sublimity. Many felt torn between the wish to be generous and compassionate, and the lust for revenge and self-assertion. For Lassalle, his last duel was all about revenge, as he had confessed to his lady-friend: "This fight is not a duel, it is pure revenge."[72] As an experienced marksman, he was sure that he would kill or hurt the opponent while he himself would escape unscathed.

Life proved him wrong, though. The fight was a duel, meaning that chances and risks were evenly distributed. It happened time and again that students without any shooting experience killed or wounded officers who were well-trained in pulling the trigger. A duel's outcome was always unpredictable, which turned it, as Lassalle had to learn as a final lesson, into an unsuitable measure for revenge.

Shaming the coward

Duels, however, offered a perfect platform to display manly character and personality. "Men of honour" as they used to call themselves, were true men who embraced the code of chivalry as much as the rules of gentlemanly behaviour. A gentleman's conduct, as defined by the *Encyclopaedia Britannica* in 1856, was "regulated by a true principle of honour, which springs from that self-respect and intellectual refinement which manifest themselves in unconstrained yet delicate manners."[73] His character was mild and his conduct inoffensive. At the same time, though, he stood up for his convictions, values and beliefs. He defended them through vigorous action and did not shy away from sacrificing his life or health for what he found important and necessary. A man of honour was, in short, anything but a coward.

The duel proved just that. Fearing for his life and avoiding any action that could put him in danger was not something of which a duellist could be accused. His whole behaviour spoke to the exact opposite. He personified courage, no more and no less. And he personified it in a special way. His courage was not the daredevilry and foolhardiness of some youngster who did not know or care about risk. Men like Humboldt, Boyen, Bismarck or Vincke, who were in their late

30s or 40s, could hardly be considered ignorant fire-brands. Rather, they were men who thought of them-selves as responsible adults, fathers and husbands, who held important public offices and made an impact on the world in which they lived. Still, they found it necessary to demonstrate courage, fully aware of the life-threatening risks involved. Courage for them was equivalent to fortitude and steadfastness. Rather than offensively moving forward and pushing their limits, they held their ground.

To stand up for one's beliefs and fight bravely was deemed, as the famous law professor Rudolf von Jhering framed it in 1872, a duty of "moral and physical self-preservation." Whoever denied a man's right to personally and forcefully fend off an offence, was "unmanly" and acted as a "moral eunuch."[74] In the same vein, Hans Delbrück, a conservative professor of history and influential author, described the "psychological undertone" of a duel as the following: "To be a whole man and personality, one needs the courage to support one's cause in person. To have that courage makes up manly honour."[75]

Thomas Mann beautifully captured and highlighted this attitude in his novel *Magic Mountain* published in 1924. Looking back at pre-war society and its cultural trajectories, he let the two intellectual antipodes,

Naphta and Settembrini, engage in a duel. Hans Castorp, the novel's main character, objected by arguing that there had been no real insult between the two but only disagreement on a "matter of abstractions." As he saw it, the latter had nothing to do with personal honour and thus did not merit a duel. Settembrini felt otherwise. For him, "things of the mind" were highly personal and contained "more possibilities of deep and radical hatred, of unconditional and irreconcilable hostility than any relation of social life." They directly and relentlessly invited the "radical intimacy" of the duel. And then he explained to his young friend what duelling was really about: It "is not an 'arrangement,' like another. It is the ultimate, the return to a state of nature, slightly mitigated by regulations which are chivalrous in character, but extremely superficial. The essential nature of the thing remains the primitive, the physical struggle, and however civilized a man is, it is his duty to be ready for such a contingency, which may any day arise. Whoever is unable to offer his person, his arm, his blood, in the service of the ideal, is unworthy of it; however intellectualised, it is the duty of a man to remain a man."[76]

In 1910, the author of this pathos-ridden paragraph had himself been confronted with such a contingency. Theodor Lessing, a 38-year-old philosopher, felt insulted by an article that Mann had written, and asked him (by telegram!), if he was prepared to defend his opinions "at gunpoint." Mann was not sure how to react and asked his father-in-law for advice. Alfred Pringsheim, a professor of mathematics, was himself an experienced duellist; as a passionate admirer of Richard Wagner, he had once physically attacked a stranger who did not share his musical sympathies, and consequently was called out. In Thomas Mann's case, however, he recommended a strategy of de-escalation. Since Lessing's challenge had not been communicated in the appropriate form, there was no need to accept it. His son-in-law gratefully accepted the advice since he was obviously not ready to "offer his person, his arm, his blood, in the service of the ideal."[77]

Not every intellectual dispute or difference of taste, therefore, had to end in a duel. It very much depended on the situation, on its publicity, on the personal character of those involved, on their sensibilities and judgments. The culture of honour, as it was practised and observed in Continental Europe until the early twentieth century held many opportunities for negotiation and compromise. The duel was but the most radical and existential solution to a conflict that had touched on men's sense of integrity. As an extreme, it brought to light and emphasized the underlying principles of honour: an intense feeling of "self-love," i.e. self-centredness and self-respect, connected to the claim of being recognised and treated accordingly by one's peers.

Equality and group cohesion

Those peers were of crucial importance. Honour was not an emotional capital that could be traded and exchanged regardless of space and social status. It was only valued by, and within, social groups that shared the same notions and practices. If, for instance, a middle-class entrepreneur got insulted by a worker, he would remain quite unconcerned. In serious cases, he might take the offender to court and have him fined or flung into prison. His personal sense of honour, though, was left unharmed. If, however, a man from his own circles dared to deny him the respect that he deemed necessary, things were different. Sociologically speaking, honour served as a means of social integration: it established certain rules of conduct within a social group and enabled its members to solve their disputes in a way that did not damage the community.

How this worked in real life can again be studied by looking at the extreme case of duelling. Above all, the duel was a social practice that relied on, and expressed the equality of its actors. They met on equal terms and fought under equal conditions. They both consented to the rules and were not taken by surprise. No one was attacked from behind, or ambushed at night. The fight took place in broad daylight and under the supervision of peers (seconds, doctors, friends). Through this setting, the opponents claimed to be men of honour belonging to the same social universe. By confronting each other on the duelling site, they acknowledged and recognized this claim. And they allowed credit for, and invested in, the cohesion of what was called "the society of those capable of giving satisfaction" (*satisfaktionsfähige Gesellschaft*).

Duellists did even more: They actively sought to maintain the respect members of that society owed to each other, and they went as far as to aim at reconciliation. This was framed in rather abstract terms by a student from a Heidelberg fraternity: He called the duel a "blood baptism," in which "the stains of hatred have been washed away, and love has prevailed over enmity." Reason, the student added, "can never understand this, but feeling knows it as an inescapable truth."[78] How this feeling was translated into action, was demonstrated time and again. Humboldt was absolutely sure that the duel with the Prussian minister of war had purified and stabilised their relationship. After the fight, they spoke "much and very well" to each other on a bridge over the Danube river, perfectly aware of the symbolism attached to the particular site.[79] Reconciliation even happened *post mortem*. In 1828, the brother of a man who had been killed in a duel, asked to pay a visit of respect to the colleague who had fired the mortal shot and who had subsequently been detained in a fortress (a prison for the privileged). Likewise, parents of duelling victims often filed clemency appeals for their sons' opponents who had been lawfully convicted to serve time in prison.[80]

These acts of sympathy testify to the general support the duel enjoyed in those circles who subscribed to honour as a crucial emotional disposition and habitus. They are hard to understand, though, by present-day men and women who have grown up in societies that no longer value this kind of gentleman's honour. In twentieth-century Europe and the US, honour lost its emotional appeal and became "meaningless."[81] Strong feelings of honour are no longer to be expected from university professors, civil servants, or the world of business and finance. Men might still be irritated when insulted, and even file a lawsuit against slander. But they would surely not be as upset as to risk their lives in a duel. The compelling emotional overtones and undercurrents of honour have disappeared. What is left is one's reputation, one's good name, the quest for recognition.[82] This is what the eighteenth and nineteenth centuries used to call "external honour." Its internal disposition that was "rooted in the heart" and made the blood boil has evidently vanished.

Crimes of honour, now and then

It survives, however, in other social groups and cultures. Present-day Western societies still know of highly ritualised and emotionally charged honour practices performed in marginal or liminal settings. The Mafia and related criminal networks are a case in point, and so are certain male adolescent milieus. While the former use honour mainly to strengthen group cohesion, the latter tend to stress self-assertive claims to honour and respect that are inextricably tied to the male body and its physical as well as sexual prowess.[83]

Non-Western societies also cherish strong notions, feelings and practices of honour tied (though not exclusively) to gender roles and male power. "Family honour" acquires a particularly urgent meaning that often results in violent and aggressive actions against female family members accused of dishonourable behaviour. According to UN reports, the number of "honour" killings is on the rise worldwide.[84] They are not confined to countries like Pakistan, Saudi Arabia or Afghanistan, but can as well be observed in Paris, London, and Berlin, in their Turkish, North-African or South Asian, mostly Muslim neighbourhoods. Usually a father or brother murders his daughter or sister respectively, because she did not lead the kind of life dictated by the family customs. She has thus offended or violated the family's honour, and the family takes revenge.[85]

Are these practices related to crimes of honour committed by upper- and middle-class Europeans some generations ago? Quite evidently, there are some important differences. For one thing, the duel could not be considered murder since it was voluntary, consensual, and symmetrical. Men were not forced to fight a duel but did so because they found it appropriate for various reasons. They met on equal terms: neither the offender nor the offended claimed advantages. They bore the same weapons, they exposed themselves to the same risk of killing and being killed. The duel was not an act of revenge or premeditated murder that left the victim no chance of hitting back or defending himself. Instead, it was a social practice that drew on, and established the equality of those involved. This implied, for another thing, that duels were fought between men only, and between men of similar social backgrounds. Duels between a man and a woman were virtually unheard of, and so were duels between men of different social classes.

LE MONDE RENVERSÉ.

Les femmes se battent en duel.

Fig 2.
Le monde renversé. Les femmes se battent en duel (detail from a 19th-century postcard).

Still, the notion of honour at stake in both cases seems to be somehow similar. First, honour holds such strong emotional power that it imperatively calls for action. Men do not just feel it, they act upon it. Second, the action is always a male prerogative. Women might lose their honour, but they can never restore it by themselves. Duelling is an exclusively male affair; it would mean *le monde renversé* if women ever took to it. Third, female honour (or family honour as it is sometimes called) is always tied to sexuality. It is about chastity, purity, and appropriate sexual behaviour. It is about not sleeping around or betraying your husband. Male honour, on the other hand, does not bear any direct sexual connotations. To a large extent, it consists of safeguarding the female honour and making sure that what belongs to him—or the family—is not taken away or sullied by someone else.

This was demonstrated to the global public in 2006 during the Soccer World Cup final. Towards the end of the game, which was won by the Italian team, the French captain Zinédine Zidane suddenly head-butted the Italian player Marco Materazzi in the chest. The referee immediately showed him the red card and Zidane left the field. Everybody wondered what had caused his violent action. Two days later, Materazzi admitted to the *Gazetta dello Sport* that he had insulted Zidane but did not say how. Shortly after, Zidane explained himself on French television. He apologized to the "two or three billion people" who had watched his "inexcusable gesture." He even apologized to Materazzi—but he did not regret what he had done. The

Italian had directed some "very hard words" at him allegedly insulting both his mother and sister. "I am a man and some words are harder to hear than actions. I would rather have taken a blow to the face than hear that." Even four years later, he was not willing to change his mind: to ask for Materazzi's forgiveness, he told the Spanish newspaper *El País*, would "dishonour me. I'd rather die."[86]

Here we hear exactly the kind of language that was spoken in eighteenth- and early twentieth-century Europe. It was also the language with which Zidane had been brought up. The son of Algerian immigrants from the Kabylie region (which Bourdieu had studied in his early ethnographic research), he was accustomed to honour as social and emotional capital that needed to be protected and maintained. Losing one's honour was worse than death. What was perceived as an insult closely resembled the list of offences that European men of honour had taken to heart: a blow to the face— above all, though, an attack on the sexual integrity of female family members. In 2007, Materazzi finally disclosed what he had said on the soccer field: he had called Zidane's sister a "puttana," a whore, and he had insinuated that he would like to take advantage of her.

If Zidane had lived a hundred years earlier and belonged to "polite society," he would have called out

Materazzi. His peers would have agreed and given him their support and solidarity. An offence as "hard" as this one could not have been redressed by any other means. Zidane shared the same notions of honour but used different practices to defend it. By taking direct physical action, he followed the example of less educated men who had long since settled their honour disputes with fists and brawls. Instead of keeping a stern face and delegating the affair to third persons who would then submit the challenge, they struck back at the offender and took immediate revenge.[87] While duellists acted in "cold blood," less "civilised" men let their blood boil. Still, it was no less a social act adhering to a commonly understood script.

Chastity and family honour

Women's sexual behaviour was a major topic when men felt their honour insulted. Especially those cultures that put a high price on female chastity held men responsible. This applies to Mediterranean societies like the one from which Zidane's family originated;[88] it also applied to noble and middle-class circles setting the tone in European societies of the long nineteenth century. While members of the lower classes apparently observed less strict rules of conduct, "good society" was obsessed with female "purity" and shame. A young factory worker could have premarital sex without being called a prostitute; she should make sure, though, that she only shared pleasures with the one who would later become her husband. In contrast, the unmarried daughter of a middle-class family had to abstain from sex altogether. Her chastity was guarded like a treasure—which had a lot to do with marriage strategy and worries about paternity. In families that had much to be inherited, paternity issues were of utmost importance. A woman who had slept around before marriage could not be trusted afterwards. In addition, the new morality of romantic love demanded exclusivity and complete devotion on the part of the female partner. In her own best interest, this should only take place in marriage which offered her long-term security and protection.[89]

Female honour thus became inexorably linked to sexual chastity. Educational treatises, advice literature, legal texts and religious sermons all worked towards pointing out the intimate connection between a woman's "moral existence" and her chastity. A woman who had lost the purity of body and soul, was deemed "fallen" and could never reclaim her honour. This was how "nature" had organised it—nature, not culture.[90] Culture only followed nature's intentions by enshrining them in social institutions and legal regulations (like the one that punished a married adulteress much harder than a married adulterer). By referring to nature, contemporaries both universalised and legitimized a moral code that was by no means natural, but integrally tied to man-made concerns and interests.

Hence, female honour and male honour were conspicuously and closely related to each another. Since men based their honour on "courage and strength" (Grevenitz), they were held in charge of protecting the honour of their female relatives considered too weak to stand up for their own integrity. This was part of the code of chivalry that was widely praised as an asset of Western civilization. Upon closer examination, however, men acted not only as protectors and guardians, but also as proprietors and representatives. The language of honour and its semantics were absolutely clear about this: attacking a woman's honour meant, in the first place, insulting her husband, father or brother. Anyone who seduced a married woman offered the "greatest affront" to her husband, according to one judge who in 1902 sentenced an adulterer for killing the deceived husband in a duel. In a similar vein, Prussian ministers of justice and war identified adultery as a sign of disrespect for the husband whose manliness and *Wehrhaftigkeit* (ability and willingness to fight) were contested by the adulterer's behaviour.[91]

This is what lay beneath the term "family honour"—a term that was harshly criticised by early feminists. They astutely regarded it as an "extended version of male honour" and pointed to the fact that it could be harmed, but not restored by women.[92] Interestingly enough, the term was even used in legal documents of the time. The 1907 Hague Convention respecting the Laws and Customs of the Land included a paragraph on "family honour." Family honour, the article said, had to be respected by military authority of an occupied territory.[93] Reading this now, we probably shrug our shoulders. But people at the time knew exactly what it meant: women should not be raped.

Rape in wartime posed a particularly difficult problem. It affronted men's honour without giving them any chance to restore it. They could neither challenge nor take on the rapist who was protected by the power of the victorious army. Instead, they were made to stand by and experience utter emasculation. This predicament was depicted in the numerous drawings and lithographs documenting "atrocités allemandes" during World War I. Many showed women raped and mutilated by German soldiers.[94] Using those atrocities as a propaganda weapon worked both ways: by denouncing and shaming the offender as someone who took advantage of weak and helpless women, the material also highlighted the dishonour of French or Belgian men who had kept in the background.

Rape, sex, and national honour

But there was another dimension that should not go unnoticed. Violating the honour of the enemy's wives and daughters was not only an attack on husbands and fathers. It was meant and perceived to target and damage the honour of the whole nation. Wartime rape thus held a highly symbolic and political meaning as much as it humiliated individual women and hurt men's self-perception.[95] In order to explain this, we have to remember the connection between social and political honour that was forged and stabilised during the modern period. The fact that nations and states were imbued with honour was a common paradigm of nineteenth-century European thought. National and state honour was deliberately moulded on the example of male honour as we have seen it developed and practised in "polite society." In the 1880s and early 1890s, Heinrich von Treitschke, an influential German historian and public intellectual, delivered passionate university lectures on slander, reparation and respect that must have sounded thoroughly familiar to his students, well-versed in the academic honour culture. "Any insult offered," he stated, "even if only outwardly, to the honour of a State, casts doubt upon the nature of the State." Therefore, "if the flag is insulted, the State must claim reparation; should this not be forthcoming, war must follow, however small the occasion may seem; for the state has never any choice but to maintain the respect in which it is held among its fellows."[96] War here was equivalent to the duel, and the "honour of a State" obviously shared many features with the honour of a gentleman.

Contemporary politics seemed to confirm Treitschke's concept of state honour. The Franco-German war of 1870–71 and its prehistory had been largely conceived of in terms of honour and shame, of humiliation and satisfaction. The attempt of the House of Hohenzollern to take possession of the vacant Spanish throne was interpreted as an attack on French *honneur*; the French government demanded a "satisfaction éclatante." Bismarck's Ems Dispatch was perceived as a "slap in the face" of the French ambassador and thus of France proper.

Paris, in turn, declared war on Prussia in order to defend French honour and interests. Prime Minister Bismarck, who had stood his ground on numerous affairs of honour, was equally concerned about the Prussian monarchy not being abased. "We can only choose between war," he told the Prussian missions abroad, "or a humiliation that the honour of the nation cannot put up with."[97] Four decades later, the outbreak of World War I was negotiated along the same semantic lines.[98]

States valuing honour and demanding satisfaction could be regarded as prolonging the absolutist tradition which had identified prince and state. Neither Louis XIV nor Frederick II had drawn a distinction between their honour as monarchs and the honour of the states they were thought to personify. Facing defeat in 1760, the Prussian king vigorously refused to sign a "humiliating peace." By implication, his "inner motivation and feeling of honour" was deemed binding and authoritative for the country as a whole.[99] Since the French Revolution, the notion of monarchical and state honour had explicitly extended to the nation comprising all (male) citizens. Each one of them was now called on to feel personally insulted by derogative acts of foreign governments and the nations they represented. This introduced an urgency and passion into foreign politics that had hitherto been unknown. The full thrust of this passion was felt in 1914, when the language of honour was not only spoken among diplomats, but also used to whip up national feelings and prepare Europeans for war.

This was immediately translated into public imagery. Female national allegories that had been popularized throughout the nineteenth century became war heroines and took up the sword. *Deutschland—August* 1914, the famous painting by Friedrich August Kaulbach, depicted Germania in full armour and flowing blond mane, ready to defend and attack. She joined German soldiers on the battlefield whenever and wherever it was necessary to uphold the "German honour."[100] But national allegories also served as icons of ridicule and humiliation.[101] The nation represented by a female figure was thus stripped of honour and respect. In turn, men were asked to defend and restore national honour by enlisting in the army and fighting for victory. As Kaulbach painted his armoured Germania in Bavaria, the British Admiral Charles Fitzgerald founded the Order of the White Feather in Kent. It encouraged women to give out white feathers—a well-known symbol of cowardice—to younger men who did not wear a uniform and had not joined the troops. This was meant as an outright humiliation, and it often had this effect.[102]

Gutless men were considered as detrimental to national honour as women who were forced, or even

Fig 3.
"Chartres, August 18, 1944" by Robert Capa.

worse, voluntarily chose to have sex with the enemy. On August 18 1944, war journalist Robert Capa took a photograph in the streets of Chartres, France. It showed a woman with her hair shorn carrying a child in her arms. The child was hers, the offspring of a relationship with a German soldier. After the liberation, she was publicly humiliated as a traitor:

she had not only lost her honour as a woman, but had also insulted the national honour by rejecting French men and instead privileging a German lover. To brand her as a traitor, fellow-citizens sheared her hair and made her the subject of public outrage and ridicule.[103]

The connection between female and national honour was witnessed all over Europe, in Denmark and Norway as much as in Czechoslovakia and Greece.[104] German women, who had been raped by (mostly) Russian soldiers, were given a hard time by their husbands who, after returning from the war, felt personally dishonoured and could not face the shame.[105] When the war was over, women who had had affairs with Allied soldiers were accused of violating the national honour ("It took six years to beat the German soldier, but it took only five minutes to win over a German woman"). *Fräuleins* who went out with an American GI were beaten up and had their hair shorn. Although economically beneficial to their families, their behaviour raised concerns about moral looseness and was interpreted as degrading German men.[106] The discourse was fraught with semantics that gendered national honour and nationalised female honour.

The decline of honour, or its return?

Has this language gone out of fashion nowadays? Has it made room for more individualised, less standard-ized and patriarchal notions of gender, nation and so-ciety? In 1973, sociologist Peter Berger wrote: "Honor occupies about the same place in contemporary usage as chastity [...] Both concepts have an unambiguously outdated status in the *Weltanschauung* of modernity [...] At best, honor and chastity are seen as ideological leftovers in the consciousness of obsolete classes, such as military officers or ethnic grandmothers."[107] This statement was obviously aimed at the US and perhaps also Europe, from where the "ethnic grandmothers" had originally come. Evidence seemed to confirm the claim. Even in countries like Germany or Italy, which had tried to restore strong notions of honour (and chastity) during fascism, the gradual decline and erosion of honour as an emotion and a social prac-tice became prevalent and could not be stopped. This was closely tied to societal transformations that were accelerated after WWI and gathered even more mo-mentum after WWII. European societies became far more egalitarian and less class-structured. The social stratification of honour that had survived the early modern period lost its legitimacy and was no longer taken for granted. Dignity started to prevail as a universal human concept superseding honour, as bound to distinctive social groups.

In contrast with dignity, honour had been inextricably linked to highly self-assertive and aggressive practices. Both in politics and social conduct, honour required violent action that often resulted in the loss of life and limb. After two devastating wars and mass murder of an unprecedented scale, Europeans were less inclined to cherish concepts of male heroism that bore the risk of death in order to prove one's valour. Embracing and enjoying life without further commitment to notions of national duty or social responsibility gained currency in post-war Western Europe.

This applied even to those groups and classes that had tenaciously stuck to exclusionary practices of honour. Being members of a *satisfaktionsfähige Gesellschaft* had put a great burden on men's actions and attitude. As "men of honour," they had to pay meticulous attention to formal rules and social conventions, and to hold death in higher regard than life. When codes of social conduct became less formal during the 1960s, a heavy blow was dealt to the *point d'honneur*—a blow whose liberating effects, however, could not be denied. Furthermore, increasing individualisation and pluralisation of styles and manners undermined the defining power of formerly dominant circles.

Equally important, gender relations underwent radical change. Women no longer accepted the iron rule dictating that their honour depended on chastity and sexual purity. They took offence at patriarchal notions of family honour lost by women's alleged weakness and rekindled by men's alleged strength. Women like Caroline von Humboldt, who in 1815 had strongly supported her husband's decision to fight a duel, were hard to find a hundred years later. When Theodor Fontane published his novel *Effi Briest* in 1895, he was puzzled by the readers' reactions. Everybody sympathised with Effi, the young woman who had had a love affair that her husband found out about years later. He challenged the lover to a duel, shot him and divorced Effi. His behaviour found little approval among Fontane's readers which caused the author to wonder about his contemporaries' "weak morals."[108] By 1974, when the book was adapted for film, moral codes had changed even more, and Fontane's ideas about male and female honour were altogether lost on the German public.

Hence there is ample evidence that honour has indeed become a "lost emotion" in twentieth-century Western societies. But how does Nicolas Sarkozy's outburst fit into the picture? What do we do with Zinédine Zidane's headbutt, and the honour killings that continue to take place in some urban neighborhoods? And how do we account for what happened during the Yugoslav wars of the 1990s? They introduced organised mass rape to the European theatre of war and used it to humiliate men and impair national honour. What had been known as more or less individualised acts of sexual violence in modern warfare developed into a strategy to foster ethnic cleansing. Rape camps were set up to impregnate women held captive and thus destroy the cultural and social ties of victims' communities.[109]

These facts cast doubt on the liberal-progressive view that sexualised notions of honour have fallen out of fashion in post-1945 Europe. Even if women no longer accept their honour to be solely identified by notions of sexual integrity, they cannot escape patterns of male behaviour targeting them as such—and, in addition, connecting their integrity to the integrity of the nation to which they belong. In circumstances surrounding violent ethnic conflict, as witnessed in former Yugoslavia (and multiple African states ever since), women have been and are still held prey as bearers and representatives of national or ethnic honour. Anyone who violates their sexual integrity, humiliates their male protectors, insults the national honour and emasculates their ethnic group.

What happened in Bosnia-Herzegovina calls into question the powerful Western narrative of female sexual liberation and emancipation. It only seems to work successfully in those regions whose inhabitants experience relative social peace and security. Highly militarized societies and those torn by war in contrast tend to quickly (re-)install notions of gendered honour that reflect older concepts of female chastity and male physical force. Wherever "obsolete classes" like military officers reclaim power, honour is back on the agenda. This is even more relevant for places where "ethnic grandmothers" hold their ground. Instead of grandmothers, however, it is mostly fathers and brothers who are obsessed with honour and tightly control their daughters' and sisters' sexuality. Here again, family honour essentially depends on female chastity which, as some immigrant groups see it, is threatened by the demoralising influence of the Western host society. The clash of cultures is thus being acted out over the female body, and honour comes at a high price. How long this price will continue to be paid, remains to be seen. If honour serves, as Georg Simmel knew, as a means to strengthen a group's internal cohesion, it gains currency when boundaries between "us" and "them," between in-group and out-group, have to be strong and impenetrable.

Those boundaries, to return to where we started from, are getting weaker and weaker within the European Union. Where states and nations before 1945 waged battles of honour against each other, honour has since then become "obsolete" as a political concept and emotional disposition among EU members. Invoking honour, as the French president did in 2010, was therefore met with widespread bewilderment. "Honneur et patrie" may still have a more vibrant sound in France where General de Gaulle held office until 1969 and continued his war-time efforts to save French national honour during the campaign against Algerian independence. Other Europeans, however, remained unmoved—like many a French citizen who felt put off by Sarkozy's agonal pathos.[110]

Chapter 2

Gendering emotions

Emotions, whether lost or retrieved, come in socially specific and culturally diverse forms. Honour, for instance, was an emotional disposition deeply ingrained in nineteenth-century European society, and yet, it took multiple shapes and translated into different practices. The latter varied according to social class, age, religion, and national belonging. Most conspicuously, they varied according to gender. Although honour was relevant to both men and women, its manifestations and meaning differed vastly. For women, honour was exclusively linked to their sex and sexual behaviour. For men, it was more socially complex and could be attacked by a wide range of offenses, from verbal insults to a slap in the face. The gravest offense, however, was also a sexual one, namely the seduction of a female family member. In such cases, husbands, brothers or fathers felt dishonoured in their own right and challenged in their quest for manliness.

Even though male honour had a sexual subtext as well, there remained a crucial gender difference. First, while it was a subtext for men, it was the main text for women. Second, men were masters of their own honour while women were not. Female honour, once impaired and insulted, could not be restored by the woman herself. Strictly speaking, it was lost forever. Even male family members could not redeem it. By calling the offender to account, they protected their own honour, since a "fallen" woman never got her honour back. In contrast, a man found ample opportunity to prove himself honourable and silence those who dared to sully the shining shield of his honour.

Honour thus provides a good example of how emotions and their related practices were gendered. Here as everywhere, gender differences, as Natalie Zemon Davis has shown in her work, are a fascinating research topic. This applies to every field, and every period of history. Emotions are no exception, as *Fiction in the Archives* has eloquently proven. When appealing for clemency, a woman who had killed her husband would give different reasons in comparison with a man who had killed his wife. While men invoked rage that had led them to retaliate against a violent wife, women preferred to speak about anguish and desperation. They did so, in Davis's view, because rage was not a proper excuse for them. Even if women were known to be furious, and legitimately so, their rage was considered harmful. It was passion rather than affect, and thus far more enduring and dangerous. While men were deemed hot and dry beings whose indignation could erupt in short fits of rage and aggression, women were thought to be cold and humid. This allowed them to harbour long-term and premeditated passions detrimental to their own well-being and that of others.[111]

Natalie Zemon Davis's stories and pardon tales were about the sixteenth century which, as the evocation of humoral pathology reveals, was still in great proximity to ancient concepts of human nature. What, then, happened when those references gradually passed into oblivion? How did modern science, as it developed from the seventeenth century onwards, change ideas about men and women, about their temperaments and character? What did it disclose about their emotions, their passions, affects, sentiments, and appetites? And how did this new knowledge shape social norms and practices?

Rage and insult

To answer those questions, encyclopaedias offer a good starting point. They began to be published at the beginning of the eighteenth century and were explicitly aimed at informing the public about any matters of interest. These included technological innovations as much as debates on moral philosophy. Encyclopaedias processed knowledge generated in all fields of empirical research and metaphysical reflection. They did so in order to enlighten readers and familiarise them with what learned men and scientists had discovered about nature and culture. At the same time, they helped to canonise certain forms and contents of knowledge (and discredit others). But they also kept pace with the dynamics of knowledge production. Unlike earlier forms of lexica, the famous *Britannica* or the German *Brockhaus* appeared in numerous editions that quickly succeeded one another and thus accounted for the rapid expansion and innovation of available knowledge.

The first German-language encyclopaedia was published between 1734 and 1754. With sixty-eight volumes and approximately 288.000 entries, it became the most comprehensive lexical project of its time. Volume sixty-three from 1750 contained a thirty-five column article on rage (*Zorn*). Forty per cent of the text dealt with the wrath of God, sixty per cent with the rage of man. The definition was gender-neutral: "Rage, in Latin, Ira, is the affect that emerges when one feels insulted, either directly or indirectly (through a person for whom one cares). The affect aims to fight off the perceived evil."[112] It is important to note that rage is seen as an affect rather than a passion. The affect enables the offended to act out, offer resistance, and force back the "evil" influence. Rage or anger clearly empowers a person and fills them with vigour. This is acknowledged by present-day psychologists who perceive anger as expressive and highly mobilising: they call it a powerful or sthenic emotion, in contrast to asthenic ones that weaken a person's energy and dampen their spirit.[113]

And where is gender? The 1750 definition did not allude to men or women. The semantics, however, did. When contemporaries talked about "feeling insulted," they implicitly talked in gendered terms. Insult, in those days, always targeted a person's honour, and honour concerned men in different ways and qualities than women. A man who felt offended had to react or would otherwise be deemed a coward, his masculinity defied. The more determination he showed, the better. Rage here acquired a downright masculine quality, as reflected in a lexicon entry from 1827 describing rage as "an affect of annoyance in its manly, vigorous expression."[114] Romantic writer Friedrich Schlegel took a similar view when he associated rage with masculinity. Women, he claimed, "know nothing about rage"; only the "*higher-minded* female character is capable of rage and thus manly.[115]" Schlegel's friend Novalis likewise thought of *les femmes* as characteristically asthenic.[116] Sthenic emotions, and in the first place rage, were non-accessible to those feeble creatures disqualified to act energetically on their own behalf. Weakness was what defined and characterised femininity. "Feminine ways are called weaknesses," noted Immanuel Kant in 1798, and popular encyclopaedias readily agreed.[117]

Power and self-control

Weakness, though, was not only associated with the absence of physical strength. It also indicated a lack of moral and social power. Since Antiquity, rage had been seen as a feature of the powerful. Only those at the top could afford and enact it. They alone had the power to let others feel their rage. This social attribution still resonated in the 1770s when the German pedagogue Johann Bernhard Basedow published his acclaimed *Elementarwerk*. It instructed parents as well as public and private teachers on how to educate boys below the "academic age." Basedow strongly advised his young pupils against feeling rage: "Do not believe that rage adds to your reputation, because noble and superior men often give themselves to rage." According to the educational reformer, rage did not procure social credit, but rather lowered the enraged person in front of others. As a cautionary tale, he mentioned the example

Fig 4.
Basedow, Elementarwerk "The furious rage of a woman; its effect on the tea table and the mirror; the servant's indiscreet laughter."

of a woman who erupted over her maid breaking a jar. "How disgusting, how abominable her gestures are!" Rather than exerting power, she ridiculed herself, just like "powerless" children did. When the latter showed rage, they were "simply laughable."[118]

There is one more aspect ushering gender into the semantics of rage. From the early modern period, and culminating in the eighteenth and nineteenth centuries, European society took a growing interest in affect regulation. As much as it was deemed necessary for a person to have and show feelings, those should be moderated and appear in a well-tempered form. Letting rage take possession of one's mind and actions was considered inappropriate, irrational and uncivilised. Instead of displaying affect and passion, and resorting to raw force, men needed to tone down their irritation and control their rage. A man should "at least be able to master his rage and avoid those words and deeds that might cause further distress." The more educated and refined he was, the better he had learnt to keep his passions under control.[119]

Here, the language was clearly and openly gendered. Self-control was something of which only adult men seemed capable. Women and children were regarded as lacking the moral willpower and discipline to moderate their affects. If their constitution was as delicate as Novalis and others assumed, it did not offer them the strength to hold back or regulate their emotions. Marin Cureau de la Chambre, who was Louis XIV's personal doctor, referred to his medical expertise when he stated in the mid-seventeenth century:

"Due to their constitution, youngsters and women do not have a strong mind and thus have to apply great effort to resist their passions." More often than not, those efforts failed, and women (as well as children) abandoned themselves to unrestrained rage.[120]

Women's strength, women's weakness

We see a paradox here: on the one hand, women were granted feelings that without doubt had an empowering effect. As Cureau de la Chambre saw it, women's uncontrolled rage came about as a "rapid torrent that cannot be stopped and that overflows with words and threats." Women here entered the stage as forceful actors who lashed out and frightened their opponents, even if their aggression was only verbal, not physical. Rage thus transformed women's weakness into strength. On the other hand, this very strength was increasingly judged inappropriate for several reasons: first, it was thought to be utterly harmful, above all to women's offspring. According to prevailing medical opinion, angry mothers who breastfed endangered their children's health. The milk would turn sour and cause convulsions which might eventually kill the baby.[121]

Second, female strength contradicted the ideology of gender characteristics that had become enshrined in a complex system of social and cultural practices since the late eighteenth century. In this ideology, women were the passive and men the active sex. Passivity, though, did not work in harmony with a sthenic emotion like rage. Rather, it accommodated sentiments of anger described as rage held back by the "feeling of impotence." Anger, as Meyer's *Conversations-Lexicon* stated in 1842, was mostly to be found in "nervous and testy" people who had been spoilt by a "slack education." Often it was accompanied by "abdominal ailments." All this was relevant to women and the "peculiarities" of their gender as contemporaries interpreted them.[122]

Third, the notion of women's rage as it had been evoked by Louis XIV's doctor, violated concepts of civilised conduct that were to gain currency throughout the nineteenth century. Self-control and "rational" behaviour ranked highly on the list of bourgeois expectations and virtues. Women who could not resist their passions thus became marginalised in a twofold way: they lost their femininity, and they lacked civility. For men, the story was somewhat different. They, too, had to comply with the expectation to hold back strong and overwhelming emotions. If they failed, they betrayed their social class and upbringing. Instead of acting like an "educated and cultivated" person, they resembled "raw creatures of nature."[123] At the same time, however, they were allowed to show what contemporaries called "noble rage." It sprang from moral indignation about evil and resulted in warding off injustice and "protecting the weak." In such cases, rage did not only legitimately relieve one's soul, but it also helped men to perform good deeds.[124]

The notion that rage could include an ethical element and thus qualify as "rational" is acknowledged by today's psychologists and philosophers as much as it was by their nineteenth-century colleagues.[125] What has changed, though, is its gendering. While earlier scripts had reserved noble rage exclusively for men, more recent lexicon entries dropped any mention of gender. This does not mean, in fact, that rage or anger have become gender-neutral in our times. Conventional wisdom still suggests "that anger is a 'male' emotion; women don't get angry, and if they do, they certainly don't show it." Even when women do feel anger, they express it differently: "Men hit and throw things more often, and women cry more often." Those gender differences bear a strong moral touch, and are institutionalised in expectations, standards of behaviour and "display rules." Thus, women who give free rein to their rage, tend to feel "uncomfortable" because they have violated a social norm.[127] Surveys show that women in Western societies smile more than men; in turn, "men's displays of anger have been reported to be both more pervasive and are generally more acceptable."[128]

Hence, stereotypical expectations about male and female emotional behaviour prevail and are in wide use. They not only structure how people perceive and judge that behaviour; they also bear an impact on how men and women feel and express their feelings. A dominant way for women to express anger is, as present-day psychologists observe, to shed tears. Tears here stand for desperation, grief, and sadness, i.e. for emotions described as passive, self-referential and asthenic. They thus perfectly fit the nineteenth-century notion of women as weak, powerless human beings. When tears are shed because of anger, aggression is turned inward rather than acted out (although it may also have an external referent who is supposed to feel guilty because of the sadness that he—or she—has caused the crying person).

The established fact that women in Western societies cry four to five times more often than men (and that they cry differently: longer and sobbing) has nothing to do with biological differences.[129] Rather, it is a cultural phenomenon that casts light on social norms, habits, and customs. It is the outcome, so to speak, of learning processes rather than genetic programming. Even though men and women have the same biological and neurological equipment to shed tears, they use it differently.

This insight points back to the early modern period when the topic "gender and emotions" was first publicly discussed. In older teachings on affects and passions, the gender issue had been conspicuously absent. In 1661, however, a French rhetoric academy posed the question of whether "women's passions are stronger than those of men." There was no consensus among those who sent in their replies: some speakers bluntly denied the proposition, others supported it. Strictly speaking, though, all participants were less concerned with how women and men experienced emotions. Instead, they focused on how they dealt with and expressed what they felt.[130]

There was a reason why. What "really" happened to people when affected by an emotion, strong or weak, short-lived or long-lasting, seemed basically impossible to tell. On the one hand, medical knowledge about what was going on within a person's body and/or soul was highly speculative and rested, above all, on observations of how the person acted. Appearances then allowed the observer to make a sound guess about the "inside." In this way, behaviour reflected temperament, and temperament referred to a specific mixture of bodily fluids. On the other hand, behaviour was also seen to depend on social rules and power relations. Since pre-modern societies were strictly socially stratified, they paid close attention to how differences were symbolically and practically performed. The display of passions and affects likewise followed sophisticated rules which varied firstly according to social rank and estate and secondly according to gender.

Modernity and the natural order

Modern societies emerging in the eighteenth century radically reversed that order. While they dynamised social differences, they naturalised gender differences. Whereas all men were supposed to be (more or less) equal, men and women were thought to be profoundly unequal. As much as their inequality was based on nature, it seemed to be eternally given and unchangeable. Social differences, in turn, were open to change and moderation. After the *Ancien Régime* had been abolished, any poor peasant could, at least theoretically, move up the social ladder to become a wealthy entrepreneur or doctor. Social mobility became part and parcel of modernity's credo, and so did meritocracy. No woman, in contrast, could ever become a man, nature forbid!

Apparently, the natural order as it was revealed and explored by modern scientists had also provided men and women with substantially different emotions. Biological and medical knowledge tried to leave no doubt that those emotions were genuine phenomena: natural facts that had nothing to do with social display rules or canonised standards of behaviour. Rather, it seemed the other way round: modernity had allegedly found the perfect way to at once accommodate and cultivate women's (and men's) natural faculties and propensities. In civil societies of the kind Europe saw gaining momentum from the late eighteenth century on, nature and culture worked splendidly together rather than against each other.

Upon closer examination, the congruence between nature and culture was thought to be achieved predominantly by the middle classes. While aristocrats appeared over-cultured, peasants and lower classes seemed prone to the "state of nature" and its animal-like "instincts," "physical impulses," and "appetites." According to French philosopher Jean-Jacques Rousseau, man had to ennoble his feelings in order to proceed to the "civil state" and become a "citizen" capable of signing the "social contract." Such a citizen should neither fall prey to his "natural" inclinations, nor master an artificial and polished "language" which was only "playing at sentiment" without feeling it. Moral and civil education, in Rousseau's view, was all about raising man above the physical or animalistic, and, at the same time, minimising the level of pretension and camouflage. It was about finding the right balance between man's nature and culture.[131]

And what about woman's nature and "civil state"? Here, Rousseau was much less committed. His famous 1762 educational treatise *Emile* did dedicate a chapter to women, since Emile needed a congenial companion. Still, Sophie's education followed a completely different trajectory. Woman, so Rousseau argued, had no place in civil society: she was made to please and be useful to man only. Since she depended on him more than he depended on her, her conduct had to speak to his sentiments and appeal to his judgments. Education should thus train her to accept constraint and compulsion from early on. A girl was to be taught to master her temper and bow to the will of others. What mattered most to a woman was chastity, and pudency. Her inner feeling led her to obey her husband and be faithful to him, as well as to tenderly care for her children.[132]

Those were, in a nutshell, Rousseau's ideas on emotional gender characteristics and relations. They were shared, in one way or another, by a great many philosophers, theologians, pedagogues and doctors who, since the late eighteenth century, had enshrined them in school curricula, sermons, advisory manuals, educational and medical texts. Normative literature as well as novels overflowed with prescriptions and propositions as to what kind of behaviour was expected of men and women. As a justification, they all referred to the natural order. Nature, so the argument went, had established a "radical difference" between men's and women's physical and mental organisation. Since it was women's natural destiny to give birth, their limbs were more delicate than men's, their nerves highly irritable, and their emotions feeble and unstable. "What we love about femininity," the eminent pathologist Rudolf Virchow stated in 1848, "is but a dependence of the ovaries." To a much higher degree than men, women seemed dominated by their sexual organs. Consequently, a "special anthropology" developed that later turned into the separate science of gynaecology. By the beginning of the twentieth century, gynaecologists could claim to be the "natural" authority on all issues that concerned women, including their social position in the modern world.[133]

Nature was hence ascribed a peremptory position in defining women's and men's purpose and status. It served to legitimise male privileges as well as constraints that barred women from higher education, from entering professions and casting their vote in political elections. At the same time, though, nature happened to be an elusive category. "In the crude state of nature," Kant argued (echoing Rousseau), the "characteristic features" of the female sex could not be recognized. As with apples and pears, only culture allowed those features to develop.[134] Social groups and strata that seemed closer to nature, often displayed a lack of culture, which educated men found disturbing. More often than not, the state of nature was associated with rawness and violent behaviour inappropriate for civil society and civilised human beings. Progress, as it would go alongside the history of civilisation, expressed itself in refined manners and self-control—and in a world that acknowledged women's special nature, allowed for a clear division of male and female spheres of action, and paid equal respect to both. By 1800 that world already seemed to be in the making. Civil society as it was envisaged and gradually practised in Europe's urban centres was thought to have correctly understood the "voice of nature" and to have translated it into a modern idiom.

Emotional topographies of gender

What did this voice say about gender and emotions? The message here was less lucid and precise. As a general rule, women were perceived as the sensitive sex while men owned a "creative mind" that privileged reason and a capacity to dissect, reflect, and abstract. Women in turn were highly impressionable and affected by all kinds of sentiments and "natural feeling." While men were capable of making "cold decisions," women were tuned to warm sympathy and mild softness. Whereas the male character displayed a certain "harshness or rigour," the female character was all gentleness and benevolence.[135] Although men, too, could harbour gentle feelings of sympathy and compassion, they were mostly given to "hot passions," thus tending to appear harsh and insensitive to other people's worries or ailments. Furthermore, their worldly lives and professions filled them with anger and sorrows that stirred their blood. The female sex, in contrast, found it easier to be well-tempered, soft-spoken, and cheerful. As Joachim Heinrich Campe, an influential educator, saw it in 1789, women's physical nature allowed them to cultivate a sunny disposition. Due to their frail and delicate nerves, they were less capable of enduring strong and deep emotions.

As a result, they were less susceptible to those griev-ous and gloomy sentiments that often haunted men. While women's minds could effortlessly move from unpleasant to pleasant feelings, men harboured their passions much longer.[136]

The notion that women were superficial, ca-pricious, unsteady, and irrational, was widespread among men who, like Rousseau, Campe or Kant, set out to define the anthropological topography of gender. But there was also a fair amount of disagree-ment. According to Rousseau, women's passive and weak nature exposed them to unrestrained passion, lust and desire. Since passions were seen as originat-ing externally and overpowering the person, women became their immediate victims. Strong and active men, in contrast, could withstand and control pas-sions far more easily. Kant, writing several decades later, seemed to share this view. Over and over again, he emphasized that man's reason helped him to mod-erate and master his passions. Passions, as such, were introduced as a male prerogative and defined as long-term and imbued with reason. Women instead were given to affect (defined as short-term and without reason).[137]

Still, how did this distinction fit Campe's observa-tion that men often held hot, irascible tempers? How could women's inherent gentleness and kindness be in harmony with the notion of affect, superficiality and capriciousness? What about women's natural propensity for "slow, hidden, withdrawn" emotions that clearly resembled Kant's idea of passion as a "river that digs itself deeper and deeper into its bed"? And how to account for the outright contradiction between Rousseau and the anonymous author who, in 1824, claimed: "Man bursts with loud desire, woman takes to calm longing"?[138]

Quite obviously, gendering affects and passions posed serious problems to philosophers, pedagogues, doctors and publishers. The lack of a consistent view was mainly due to the fact that the world of emotions appeared extremely diverse and complicated. Apart from affect and passion, it consisted of appetites, desires, drives, sentiments, sensations, humours, and moods. Making sense of all those, and specifying their connection to gender, was more than even Kant could manage. Still, he tried his best. With regard to the concurrent tide of sensibility, he distinguished, as many others did, between the right and the wrong kind. "Good" sensibility went along with proper judgment and was deemed "manly"; "bad" sensibility (*Empfindelei*) by contrast was sheer weakness, "silly and childish," since it allowed oneself to be affected "by sympathy for others' condition" in a "merely passive way."[139] Passivity, as we saw earlier, was clearly more relevant to the female sex.

Sensibility

Passivity was also what critics of sensibility feared for the male sex. They condemned men who gave themselves over to reading sentimental novels and weeping over broken flowers and captured butter-

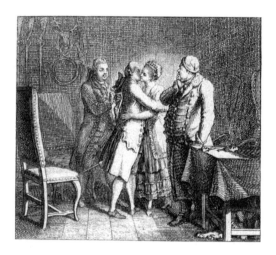

Fig 5.
Front-page vignette by Daniel Chodowiecki illustrating *The Sorrows of Young Werther*.

flies. In fact, those novels—Samuel Richardson's *Pamela* (1740) and Clarissa (1748), Rousseau's *Julie ou la Nouvelle Héloise* (1761) and Johann Wolfgang Goethe's *Die Leiden des jungen Werther* (1774), among many others—had drawn large numbers of enthusiastic readers. Women and men alike identified with the heroes and heroines and were moved to tears by their unhappy fate.[140] Such an excess of feeling, though, seemed to threaten men's masculinity, turning them into women or "eunuchs." Fathers were thus well-advised to put a stop to the *Werther* "epidemic" and instead teach their sons how to become real men and "useful citizens." This implied "stifling pain, enduring hardship, resisting danger, in one word, beating the needs of one's own flesh and blood." Bad sensibility in Kant's terms, feminine tenderness and whimpishness, were incompatible with holding public office since the latter called for "reason, seriousness, courage, and strength," i.e., genuine manliness.[141]

Hence, men increasingly distanced themselves from sensibility. Nineteenth-century authors associated it almost exclusively with women and defined it as "one of the noblest assets of the female heart." Nevertheless, they warned women against mistaking sensibility for sensitivity translated as "frenzied feeling" and "abnormal agitation of the senses." Especially since women's feelings were supposed to be more lively and subtle than men's, they had to be filtered through reason and thought. It was not enough to be sensitive, as Kant had described women's character and virtue, because this put them on a par with animals. Being human meant supplementing sense with sensibility, to invoke Jane Austen.[142]

Although not completely devoid of reason, women's nature tied them to feelings both more elementary and more passive. "Susceptibility, irritability, compassion, patience and noble weakness are the sources of female sentiments," a lexicon author wrote in 1835. Even if men and women basically shared the same emotions and passions, their "lifestyles" were so far apart as to make them "feel differently." Women's feelings were less destructive, finer, and softer.[143] Emotions like shame seemed to suit them better than men; conversely, rage would thwart their natural decency and delicacy. Women, the *Brockhaus* stated in the 1850s, "represent love and shame," men "honour." In other words, "man is conquered more by rage, fume and fury, woman by ruse, jealousy and melancholy."[144]

Emotional gender features and differences as they had been discussed in detail since Rousseau's and Kant's times remained surprisingly stable throughout the nineteenth century. The "special anthropology" reserved for women engaged with emotions, sentiments, affects and passions to a much higher degree than the male standard model. A popular illustrated lexicon from 1837 reserved the benefits of grace, tenderness, patience, sweet temper, shamefacedness and "foreboding mindfulness" for women. Yet when it came to "reason, willpower, audacity," women ranked behind men. A 1904 edition simply claimed: "Women are governed by emotion and a sentimental mind, men by intellect and reason."[145]

This did not mean, however, that men were to be purely rational beings. Even if they were called upon to apply reason and prudence before making decisions and taking action, they would be ill-advised to discard emotion altogether. Those who did were considered as deficient as those who let emotion overpower them. In 1884, a "healthy and manly character" was understood as essentially needing "capability and openness for all kinds of higher feelings. This has to go along with the ambition to get a clear idea about what is at stake in those feelings. Somebody who lacks this capability and openness is called numb and insensitive."[146]

Being called numb and insensitive was not what middle-class men strove for. It was either associated with "natural crudeness" resulting from "bad breeding, dire conditions and vulgar morals," or with a certain bluntness or smugness often associated with "excessive or over-refined pleasures of life." Faced with those daunting alternatives, men of the educated bourgeoisie chose rather to cultivate "higher feelings." This allowed them neither to be regarded as an unmanly *Gefühlsmensch* whose thoughts and actions were driven by emotions only, nor to change over to the other camp: that of the "cold" and calculated *Verstandesmensch*.[147] As early as 1795, Friedrich Schlegel had demanded "soft masculinity" (alongside independent femininity).[148] There is evidence that this softness was not just praised and propagated, but also practiced.

Romantic families, passionate politics

Especially during the first half of the nineteenth century, many doctors, lawyers and businessmen were eager to pursue domestic bliss and cherished their wives and children. They fell madly in love and talked eloquently about the "ecstasy of romantic love." Although women were regarded as guardians of love, men, too, spoke of and enacted love in a passionate and consuming way. The family became an intimate and quasi-sacred space, and was imagined as a heaven of sincere affection and authentic feeling. Here, religious rituals were performed by men and women alike. Even if women were particularly taken to tears and constantly conjured up emotions, their husbands readily joined in. As much as private Christian religion developed into a highly emotionalised social practice, both genders participated in its rituals of praying, singing and reading.[149]

For some observers, the cult of the happy family was actually too much. As early as 1810, the French aristocrat Madame de Staël half-criticised the German (protestant) habit of turning love into a "religion" and "a sort of secular service."[150] In 1846, Carl Welcker, a liberal academic and politician, mocked the "bestial family love" advocated by the German middle classes. It made him fear for the country's political culture: the emotional focus on the private sphere and domestic bliss, he argued, kept men away from the public sphere. Instead of fulfilling the "supreme and holiest duties" of a citizen, electoral delegate and lawmaker, German philistines (*Spießbürger*) and civil servants preferred to sacrifice those duties on the altar of family love. Patriotic politics were lost on them, and the fatherland left emasculate, subservient to foreign domination and internal despotism.[151] In a similar vein, Professor Karl Hermann Scheidler, who as a student had participated in the liberal-national Wartburg festival of 1817, later complained about the "dark side of our German *Gemüthlichkeit*." He located that strange sense of community and cosiness, first, in contemporary student fraternities (different from those he had joined in his early years) and, second, in the "small world of the family" that was idealised above all things. Both inevitably led to "political apathy" and a widespread reluctance to get involved in social action.[152]

That reproach, however, was overstated. The political movements of the 1830s and 1840s had mobilised hundreds of thousands of middle-class men to join clubs and associations, sign petitions and raise money, participate in demonstrations and march on the streets advocating liberal democracy and the nation-state. Conservative-minded citizens also got organised, and so did socialist workers campaigning for social rights. Even before 1848, men had not been as obsessed with family life and soft masculinity as Welcker and others claimed. The wars of the early nineteenth century had triggered emotions that had nothing to do with domesticity and marital intimacy. In the place of paternal love, they elicited love for the fatherland, and hatred towards the enemy. Propagandists on all sides appealed to patriotic sentiments and xenophobic feelings. Writers such as Ernst Moritz Arndt (who in 1848 became the senior president of the first German national parliament) lashed out against the French and condemned them for being "mean, lascivious, ravenous and cruel," for defiling German women and poisoning men's honour. German men were called to war in order to wipe out the "disgrace" and rekindle "German love, fidelity, and militancy."[153]

When the Napoleonic wars were over and German honour restored, those collective and publicly shared emotions subsequently shifted to domestic politics. Welcker drew on the analogy in 1838, when he used the term "war" literally (war with weapons) as well as metaphorically (war about political rights). Both were fought with a passion that left no man untouched. The struggle for a liberal constitution, male suffrage and responsible government pitted party against party, faction against faction. Emotions surged up that had never been encountered in former times. Instead of being obedient subjects and paying reverence to prince and king, citizens now self-confidently engaged in tough negotiations with the monarchy. They threatened to withdraw their trust and loyalty, and they referred to a new kind of love: for fatherland and nation rather than for the monarch himself. Still, the "war about rights" was not only waged between the latter and his rebelling subjects. It also took place horizontally, among citizens who held different views on the form those rights should take and how evenly or unevenly they were to be distributed. Political quarrels bore a high level of heat and noise, violent conflicts and passionate dispute. Men were insulted and physically attacked because others disagreed with their opinions, and in some cases, political opponents were assassinated.

The fact that passions played such an important role in modern politics was the reason why the latter should be reserved for men only. This was Welcker's main concern in the 1830s when he reflected on gender relations and the status of women. Due to their "mild, soft nature," women were in no position to mix with politics. Should they decide to take their chances, they would inevitably be crushed by the more passionate men while they risked losing their lovely femininity and charm. Here, the conventional argument got turned upside down: instead of linking women to emotions and men to reason, the author perceived men as passionate beings driven by "rage, defiance, and impatience." By contrast, women were imagined as smooth and gentle, showing "temper and feeling" rather than passion and affect. They were good at tolerating and enduring, whereas men went with their heads against the wall.[154]

It is not altogether clear whether the liberal professor actually approved of men's passionate behaviour in politics, or if he judged it inappropriate. On the one hand, it violated the rules of emotional restraint to which educated middle classes were well-advised to adhere.[155] On the other hand, it was commonly understood that "great deeds" came out of "great passions." "All great men" were "more or less passionate men" since "mental power, as much as organic power, from time to time needs a strong stimulus and impulse." But if exceptional achievements and triumphs were often triggered by passions, the latter should and could, under certain conditions, be accepted as morally sound.[156] For contemporaries like Welcker, who put all his energy into promoting liberal principles and a constitutional order, politics was certainly a cause meriting passionate commitment—at least for men, and men only.

What happened when eternal laws of nature were neglected and women were allowed to exert powerful and empowering emotions could be observed during the French Revolution. To many a sceptic, it had turned women into those horrible "hyenas" immortalised in Friedrich Schiller's famous *Song of the Bell*. Published in 1799, the poem found strong words and images to condemn the "uproar" of the people fighting for freedom. Women, as Schiller saw it, had behaved in a particularly outrageous way. Driven by "blind rage," they "change into hyenas / And make a plaything out of terror, / Though it twitches still, with panthers teeth, / They tear apart the enemy's heart."

For Schiller as much as for Welcker, revolutions that let women take an active political stance allowed them to mutate into wild beasts thus ultimately becoming a threat to humanity. Equally unacceptable were those *enragées*, who, though in a less violent form, demanded a share in political debates and decisions.[157] To grant women political rights was tantamount to denouncing their natural calling and social order. Passionate election campaigns or disputes in parliament, men argued, would harm femininity and put the fatherland in danger. Healthy and well-respected women would never want to participate in those flaming struggles, but would leave them to their husbands, fathers and brothers. Still, this did not rule out women becoming educated and publicly involved. According to liberal opinions, they should be allowed to listen to political debates, follow court trials, attend university lectures, establish associations and publish newspapers in support of "legitimate, worthwhile public causes." Women were out of place, though, in those arenas where political (and military) power had to be passionately fought for, gained and defended.[158]

Intense emotions versus creative minds

Women were also out of place in other areas, such as music. "Why is it," asked the famous Viennese critic Eduard Hanslick in 1854, "that women, who are by their nature inclined towards emotions, cannot achieve anything when it comes to composing music?" He gave the answer himself: precisely because the "intensity of emotions cannot dictate a musical composition. It is not emotion that composes music, it is the particular, musically trained artistic talent"—a talent women were supposedly lacking. They could, in the right circumstances, develop a performing virtuosity, interpreting pieces of music in a sensible manner. But they would never be capable of creating those pieces.[159]

Hanslick's argument was somewhat different from Welcker's. When he dismissed women's contribution to art, he sided with ideas about men's innate activity and women's innate passivity. In order to produce outstanding work, a person needed not only talent, but also discipline, willpower and energy, all inherent in men's physical and mental apparatus. Conversely, women seemed too dependent on their frail body and susceptible to their emotions to accomplish anything impressive in the arts and sciences. Imaginative creativity was thus reserved for men, as they could cultivate and combine talents, intellect and discipline free of any physical and emotional constraints.

How deeply embedded and widespread these ideas about gender difference were, came to the fore in the 1890s. More than a hundred German university professors, teachers and authors were interviewed and asked if they considered women to be capable of attending university and successfully starting a career in the professions or academe. If at all, most men could not imagine women as scientists or in any higher and independent position. At best, women were thought eligible for jobs in which they assisted men rather than pursuing their own research or professional work. Theologians saw women as inept in analysing dogmatic or historical problems because they were overly "intuitive." In law, women were found too emotional and self-righteous; as judges, they lacked the appropriate character: "They are too soft, and have too little energy to wield the sword of justice," "they tend to sentimentality" and suffered "from an abundance of feeling" that made them follow their "compassion" rather than "legal logic." In medical practice, women proved unable to use their brains independently of their emotions; they could neither reach decisions quickly nor take a strong responsible line. As women's pronounced emotionality directly affected their blood vessels and consecutively led to erratic fluctuations in the brain's blood flow, the latter caused "vertigo, dizziness, convulsion, and tremor." Altogether, they inevitably reduced women's "intellectual clarity" disqualifying them from any serious academic work[160].

Nevertheless, there were other professions that might benefit from female inclinations and feminine virtues. Nursing or educating young children were deemed a perfect fit for women precisely because of their inherent sensibilities. Women were also thought to be at their element with charities or when working in the customer services sector. Industrial labour, in contrast, posed a threat on women's health and sensitivity. Most people (men and women alike) agreed that women were ideally suited to family life. This was the sphere where their physical and mental "nature" would unfold and thrive. Here they could "represent love" and gently care for their husband and children. The family was, as democrat Jacob Venedey wrote in the 1840s, a "school of emotions": "Without family, emotions cannot develop, without emotions, there is no family." Mothers occupied centre stage: they taught their children how to feel and what to feel; they taught them love, morality, and friendship.[161]

Schools of emotions: The media

Yet, the maternal lessons were different for boys and girls, and they were not the only ones. *L'éducation sentimentale* took place in numerous institutions and with the use of various media. Novels, for instance, were thought to make a considerable impact on the manner in which male and female readers ordered and organised their "emotional economy." They provided role models, typologies and stereotypes, but they also offered bemusement and reflection. Rather than vesting their protagonists with one dominant feeling, the modern social novel as it was invented in France and Britain (less so in Germany) presented a full panoply of different and alternating emotions. As much as the narrator immunised himself against those and privileged a cold diagnostic view on his heroes and heroines, the latter usually stumbled from one to the other, always in search of true, strong and deep feeling. This fate was suffered by Emma Bovary just as it was by Frédéric Moreau, whose sentimental education, as Gustave Flaubert claimed, represented the "moral and emotional history" of his own generation.[162]

122

Whether this claim was legitimate is open to further investigation. As a general rule, novelists could not help but be close observers of contemporary mores and habits. At the same time, though, they took their distance. They chose to highlight some issues and downplay others, they radicalised certain behavioural syndromes and neglected what did not fit their argument. As to their readers, very little is actually known about how they received the message and what it meant to their own sense of belonging and being in the world. Suffice it to say that literature, both highbrow and popular, was seen as a crucial medium of educating emotions. Along with theatre and opera, it was thought to move its audience and evoke (*emovere*) appropriate feelings. Since the early modern period, plays, even more than poems and literary texts, had sought to impress men and women with affections that apparently travelled faster in the company of theatre-goers than in the more isolated act of reading.[163]

In the course of the nineteenth century, rising rates of literacy and the expansion of cultural markets made novels and plays available to more and more people. Even men and women of the lower classes, whose literary canon had formerly been monopolised by the bible and religious calendars, increasingly took to reading. While women preferred (romantic) novels, men favoured history books, science and war stories.[164] In the twentieth century, movies and, later, TV extended the consumption of cultural commodities to a degree that had been inconceivable in earlier times. What this meant for the education of feelings and its gendered practices has hardly been discussed, let alone analysed in any detail. While the cultural market's growing diversity makes it difficult to identify clear pathways and trends, research on reading patterns reveals a stunning continuity. Women still give preference to what nowadays is called human interest stories while men rather turn to newspapers, professional journals, or historical biographies.[165]

Self-help literature

What has become attractive to both genders is the genre of self-help literature promoted on the modern book market. The range of topics is huge: from breastfeeding to financial investment, from how to improve one's emotional intelligence to simplifying one's life. Some of these advisory manuals target men or women exclusively, but the majority figures as unisex literature and is relevant to both. The type of guidebook which is explicitly gendered and addresses either male or female concerns is harder to find on bookshelves today. On closer inspection, though, it still exists. *Von Tag zu Tag* (From Day to Day), for example, a book for girls in puberty, now available in its 33rd edition, was first published in 1954. From the first page to the last it spoke a highly gendered language of emotions.

In the beginning, there was the imperative: "Let us remain graceful!" The manner in which grace (*Anmut*) and beauty were defined, needless to say, referred to women only. Further on, "woman above all" was advised to continuously cultivate her sensibility and use the "fine compass of feeling" to align matters of everyday-day life. A paragraph on "The Miracle of Life" cautioned the female teenager not to let herself get carried away by "confused feelings" but to wait for the one and only who would eventually prove worthy to found a family. The chapter on "planning" mentioned how important it was for a young woman to have a job, and recommended a brochure on "313 female professions." It also emphasized that those professions were solely meant to keep women busy before they became mothers since "children completely solicit their mother's attention for a long time." Even as mothers, though, women should know about the world, read the daily paper and be informed about politics. Since male and female spheres were no longer as wide apart as in former generations, men and women were supposed to meet on an equal footing. "At home, the husband expects the wife to be his equal, especially since he knows that she often has a much more reliable sense of handling people and situations."166

Fig 6.
Three editions of *Von Tag zu Tag. Das Große Mädchenbuch* (1954, 1961, 1972).

The long-standing message about women's particular sensibility and their finely tuned emotions was thus still present in the 1960s, though in a mitigated and less explicit form. That message had been a regular feature in the great number of advice manuals published since the late eighteenth century.

While the prototypical *Knigge* had deliberately addressed a purely male audience, manners books for women followed suit. Even if they increasingly differentiated their target group according to age, religion, and class, they all conveyed a picture of the female sex as highly emotional but softly-spoken. The role model was and remained the woman who always appeared well-tempered, cheerful, and positively engaged. Such characteristics obviously did not come naturally but had to be nourished by way of constant self-inspection and scrutiny. Self-control was writ large, especially among the middle classes. Time and again, women were warned not to lash out against maids and servants and in any event to keep their emotional balance.[167]

Men received different directions. First, their emotions seemed to matter less and did not figure as prominently as women's. Second, men's reading habits rapidly moved away from *Knigge*. From the 1870s onwards, German middle-class boys were given a copy of Wilhelm von Kügelgen's *Jugenderinnerungen eines alten Mannes* on the occasion of their confirmation.[168] This nationalised version of *éducation sentimentale*, however, was soon supplemented and then replaced by a completely different genre. 1880 saw the first edition of *Das Neue Universum* which became enormously popular during the twentieth century. As a yearbook for "maturing youth" regardless of religion or class, it merged science and adventure, technological knowledge and entertainment. An appendix told boys how to apply that knowledge at home, and contained instructions for experiments—in 1910, the construction of a steam engine; in 1929 radio supplies and loudspeakers.[169]

Emotions were very much on the *Universum*'s agenda although they were not openly addressed. Emotional education worked silently, by eliciting excitement and wonder, provoking curiosity, assuring juvenile readers that everything was feasible and achievable if they had wits, discipline, and willpower. The series sought to build self-confidence, a firm belief in continual progress and in (Western) man's capacity to master any problem whatsoever. The world was there to be conquered, and the universe to be explored and exploited. Life was a hard struggle, and boys prepared for that struggle from early on.[170]

More schooling: Armies, peer groups, politics

The emphasis on toughness, discipline and daring was further strengthened in all-male institutions like the military. Under Continental Europe's regime of general conscription, every young man was a potential recruit. Each year, millions entered the "school of manliness" as it was aptly named around 1900, and continued their emotional education. They were taught to love the fatherland and be ready to sacrifice their lives in its defence. They learned to obey orders and not flinch from danger or unpleasant duty. Being called a "sissy" was the worst thing that could happen to a soldier. What should appeal to him instead was the comradeship of his peers with its typical blend of support, repression and control.[171]

Peers proved equally important in civil life, and they played a huge role in boys' (and girls') emotional coming of age. Youth groups, be they religious, political, paramilitary or independent, became a crucial factor of male socialisation. While journeymen's associations and student fraternities had existed long before, organisations for younger and adolescent boys did not emerge until the late nineteenth and early twentieth centuries. They cultivated emotional codes valuing warm and trusting relationships among their members while marking strict boundaries towards those outside that did not belong. Homoerotic feelings, more or less concealed, were part and parcel of all-male groups. Sensibility had its share, with lyrical texts sung around the campfire. At the same time, though, self-hardening and an intolerance of unmanly conduct were taken to heart.[172]

Those features gained further currency in totalitarian regimes and movements flooding Europe mostly in the wake of World War I. Italian *Fascismo, Action Française* and Vichy, *Falange Española*, the Hungarian Arrow Cross Party, and German National Socialism all preached the gospel of male harshness. Adolf Hitler imagined his young followers to be "fast as greyhounds, tough as leather and hard as Krupp steel."[173] Nazi youth organisations were eager to achieve this goal and educate boys (and later girls) in the strict racial spirit of a conquering *Volk*. What its self-proclaimed elites could accomplish was highlighted by *Reichsführer* Heinrich Himmler in October 1943. Speaking to SS officers in occupied Poland, he defended the extermination of Jews as a political necessity that had to be performed in a personally detached and machine-like fashion. "Most of you will know what it is like when a hundred corpses lie together, when there are five hundred, or when there are a thousand. And to have seen this through, and—apart from exceptional cases of human weakness—to have remained decent, has made us hard and is a page of glory never mentioned and never to be mentioned." Although the killing had been a "most difficult task" that made men "cringe" (*schaudern*) because of its sheer monstrosity, it had to be carried out "for the love of our people." In conclusion, "we have suffered no injury or damage in our inner being, in our soul, in our character."[174]

Hitler's most "willing executioners," to quote Daniel Goldhagen, were thus endowed with emotions of two sorts: They held strong positive feelings towards their comrades, their people, and, of course, towards their *Führer*. They harboured equally strong but negative feelings towards those they considered enemies and traitors. Those latter emotions, however, as Himmler made crystal-clear, had to be overcome so that they would neither get in the way of personal decency nor obstruct political logic and necessity. Neither hatred nor compassion was appropriate in completing the monstrous task. Even professional killers had to learn how to become hard and unemotional, to block out empathy, lust or rage and to perform their job as matter-of-factly as possible.

Himmler's speech was supposed to be highly confidential. It did not address the wider German public whose emotional attitudes, as the Reichsführer SS knew only too well, could not be trusted in those matters. At the same time, though, that wider public was also undergoing a complex process of emotional re-education. The Nazi regime (and fascism generally, as could be observed in other European countries) tried to evoke and manage the citizens' feelings in an unprecedented manner. Love, pride, devotion, and trust were continuously appealed to and put on stage. As a general rule, those emotions were painstakingly ritualised and regulated. Preferably, they were displayed in large crowds, as at party and mass rallies. Grandiose theatrical staging including sophisticated light and sound shows helped participants to express and experience strong feelings—which, however, should never get out of control. On the contrary, their orderly and uniform performance was to defy what had already worried the ancients: emotions' unruliness and unpredictability.

Collective emotions and charismatic leadership

Arousing affects and passions in order to move an audience to take certain actions had featured in political rhetoric ever since Aristotle's times. It was equally important, though, to effectively master and direct those emotions. Not coincidentally, the French noun émeute bears a close linguistic relation to emotion and is still used to describe a violent spontaneous manifestation mirroring collective emotions.[175] Especially when performed in a crowd, those emotions could develop a thrust that went beyond anyone's control. Liberals writing about passionate disputes in the 1830s, had no clue what was to happen to the political theatre during the era of mass politics. From the second half of the nineteenth century, more and more men voted in elections and participated in mass movements. Emotions were soon discovered to be powerful motivators and homogenizers. They mobilized citizens and attuned them to the "domestic warfare" (Churchill, echoing Welcker) that often turned election campaigns "savage."[176]

Emotions also helped to resuscitate the figure of the male leader and saviour, whose charisma largely rested on his ability to speak to the emotions of his followers. What has been called the Second Thirty Years War—the period between 1914 and 1945—brought to the fore an impressive number of charismatic leaders: Hitler, Mussolini and Stalin, alongside politicians like Churchill and Roosevelt. While pluralistic democracies like Great Britain or the USA, though, could never quite regulate and streamline the passions they aroused and kindled, totalitarian regimes like Italy, Germany, and the Soviet Union had a much firmer grip on their citizens' emotional economy. Against the background of violent repression, they employed sophisticated propaganda techniques to whip up and sustain emotions without ever losing control over them.

133

To a large degree, their success in the field of emotional politics was due to the manner in which they gendered it. Women and children were called upon to show unconditional love and reverence for the charismatic leader. Their enthusiasm, sincere or not, was publicly orchestrated and broadcast: they waved their arms, threw flowers, shouted, and cried. Men, by contrast, were sworn in to be loyal and obedient followers, marching in columns, showing hard-nosed, motionless faces that exhibited utmost determination and dedication. Their emotions were staged to be completely in sync with what the regime demanded: never unruly, always ready to spur actions that would demonstrate the efficiency and self-assertion of totalitarian politics.

In one way or another, these stagings reproduced traditional patterns of gendered emotions: women (and adolescents) who were supposed to be more emotional anyway, could display their positive feelings openly and without restraint. Their emotional outbursts and exuberance conveniently testified to the public approval (and celebration) of the regime and its *Führer*. By contrast, men held back their emotions, controlled their passions and proved that they were capable of doing whatever had to be done without flinching. They were as hard on themselves as on others, *hommes machines* and efficient tools of mass murder. This went along with the deliberate revival and strengthening of emotional dispositions like honour and shame. As mentioned before, the regime purposefully appreciated the currency of honour both in racial and in gendered terms. German (i.e. non-Jewish) women who had a Jewish lover were shamed in public and accused of racial defilement. German men in similar cases were spared the public humiliation.[177]

Was there anything new about the way in which Nazism gendered emotions? Even if the regime only seemed to continue along a familiar line, it structured and radicalised it to an unforeseen extent. For one thing, girls and women became heavily involved in the public sphere. With some delay, girls were made to join youth associations and take part in the political theatre that had largely been closed to them before 1933. Women got organised as well and took over positions of responsibility that rendered them highly visible beyond the "small world of family, home and racial reproduction."[178] For another thing, the emotional capital women invested in these public appearances was closely monitored, managed, and exploited. Never before had women's emotions—and their open manifestations—mattered so much to a government and its propaganda apparatus. Although National Socialism perceived itself as a purely male and masculine movement, it paid increasing attention to women's passionate reverence and support. The propaganda media were full of photographs and newsreels that showed women cheering the *Führer* and offering him their babies to kiss.

Fig 7.
Left: Sudeten German women welcome Hitler, October 1938.
Right: Overview of the mass roll call of SA, SS, and NSKK troops. Nuremberg, November 9, 1935.

New emotional profiles and social change

Seen in a more long-term perspective, Nazism was both advanced and retrograde in its attempt to use and channel women's emotions. Taking advantage of their public presence it capitalised on the inter-war trend of turning women into citizens, granting them political rights and recruiting them to political parties and associations. Even if citizenship and political rights were largely reduced to passive compliance (for women as well as men), women enjoyed a degree of public participation and political mobilisation unknown in the Weimar republic let alone in the political culture of the Imperial period. On the other hand, Nazism did not support the trend to level differences between male and female emotionality. Here, the 1920s had seen some initial steps. While a 1908 lexicon still emphasised women's greater "emotivity," an article in 1932 detected a growing discrepancy between younger and older generations. Young women preferred markedly clear and down-to-earth reasoning, while older women responded more emotionally.[179]

The new emotional profile of younger women corresponded to the social, economic, and cultural changes that had occurred since the beginning of the twentieth century. In many European countries, women's employment rates were on the rise, particularly in the expanding white-collar and service sector. While far away from closing the gender gap, it still allowed women to experience new challenges and freedoms. At the same time, single-sex institutions like the army or universities had either lost their prestige or were forced to include women. For some observers, the 1920s witnessed the birth of the "new woman" and the "new man." Looking back in 1941, the Vienna-born author Stefan Zweig commented on the veritable "revolution" in gender relations that had taken place during his lifetime. Forty years earlier, men and women had lived in polar emotional worlds. Men were supposed to be "vigorous, chivalrous, and aggressive," and women "shy timid, and on the defensive." Adolescent girls were kept ignorant regarding sexual issues, a fact which made them even more "curious, dreaming, yearning, and covered them with an alluring confusion." When a young man greeted them on the street, they blushed "full of shame" as if the other had found out "how much their bodies yearned for a tenderness of which they knew nothing clearly." This had all changed, at least Zweig thought so: "are there," he asked rhetorically, "any young girls today who blush?" Instead, the new generation of women "steeled" their bodies through sports and moved easily among men, without shame. They considered each other as companions sharing work, study and pastimes.[180]

With respect to young women's physical and emotional habitus, Nazism did nothing to turn back the clock, despite its ideological claims to the opposite.

Nevertheless, it took great care to emphasise gender differences: first by staging women as overly enthusiastic and emotional, second by transforming young men into well-trained labour and party soldiers and, later, efficient war machines. When the war was over and men got demilitarised, the trend towards increasing gender equality continued. This was reflected, among others, in the advice literature and etiquette books mentioned above, as well as in encyclopaedias. In 1954, the West German *Brockhaus* boldly declared the long-standing view that women's actions, more than men's, were emotionally determined, to be simply "false."[181]

The *Brockhaus* also condemned Nazism's emotional politics. To "disinhibit the masses' passions" was altogether "reprehensible" and invited a "fanaticism" that proved utterly destructive. In fact, National Socialism had welcomed such fanaticism as a highly desirable means of collective mobilisation. In 1937, its lexical definition read as follows: "a feeling of being completely immersed in, and penetrated by, an idea, a religion, a conviction, a role model or a doctrine that inspires unconditional service and commitment, if necessary by sacrificing life and limb." Fanaticism in this positive sense was "best exemplified" by the "National Socialist who does all he can do for the *Führer* and his idea."[182] It went without saying that this person was male.

Angry young men, angry young women

Later generations of men shied away from sacrificing life and limb for an idea, a doctrine or a charismatic leader. Those who had experienced a fanatic education as boys or teenagers felt betrayed and kept their distance. Some of them turned into "angry young men," who first made their appearance in Britain, following John Osborne's 1956 play *Look Back in Anger*. Dissatisfied with British upper and middle-class society, irritated by the persistence of class distinctions and proud of their lower-class mannerisms, this intellectual movement of playwrights and novelists dominated the literary mood of the 1950s and early 1960s expressing a generation's "dissentience" with "majority sentiments and opinions."[183] In West Germany, meanwhile, *zornige junge Männer* (angry young men) took to the streets and protested against rearmament, nuclear weapons, neo-fascist movements and hierarchical structures in universities. They were joined by *zornige junge Frauen* (angry young women) who eventually turned their rage against men and accused them of patriarchal repression. Reacting in an openly aggressive way by speaking out, using explicit language and throwing tomatoes clearly moved them beyond traditional gender stereotypes. Rage here acquired an empowering quality—and was accordingly frowned upon by those who, like Friedrich Schiller two centuries earlier, did not like women to become "hyenas."

What did the *enragées* of the 1970s accomplish? As much as feminism has succeeded in delegitimising gender inequality and women's discrimination, it failed to eradicate beliefs and practices which keep those inequalities alive. The fact that women still feel bad about being angry, that they take to tears rather than scream or hit, that they cry much more frequently and intensely, that they express pride less than men do, has nothing to do with biology, blood vessels, genes, or neurons. The concept of women's "special anthropology" dominating their physical and emotional apparatus clearly went out of fashion.[184]

Nevertheless, cultural modes, patterns of socialisation and self-perception are still deeply gendered. This reflects the impact of social institutions which exploit and manipulate those patterns for their own purposes. The modern workplace is a case in point. Women's jobs, much more than men's jobs, are heavily involved in emotional labour. Managing one's emotions so that they conform to occupational or organisational display rules has become particularly relevant for the ever-expanding service sector. Waitresses and flight attendants, nurses and cashiers, secretaries and saleswomen all do "service with a smile" conveying friendliness and a personal touch. Women's positive emotions are thus manipulated and commercialised in order to cheer up the customers and keep them satisfied.[185]

Fig 8.
"Service with a smile" campaign.

As argued in this chapter, such feeling and display rules have been carved out and shaped since the late eighteenth century. With the emergence of modern civil society, affects and passions became not only closely observed and regulated, but also deeply and uniformly gendered. As much as certain emotions (like shame) pertained more or less exclusively to women, others (like rage) were men's monopoly. Both

142

genders, to be sure, had emotions, even though differing in intensity and substance. The "unemotional man" did not exist. His emotional experience and behaviour were as closely monitored as a woman's. Still, they followed different norms and prescriptions.

Winds of change

Those norms and rules were embedded in, rehearsed and enhanced by social institutions, practices and media that heavily influenced men's and women's self-concepts and behaviour. Yet, this influence was not altogether determinist and left room for individual and collective agency. First, norms and related practices were challenged by those who opposed their oppressive weight. This occurred around 1800 when romantic writers revolted against what they perceived as cold, sober, machine-like bourgeois manners and feelings. In France, at about the same time, public intellectuals questioned the political grip of "Jacobin sentimentalism" and wished to limit it to the private sphere of family and friendship. Being restricted to this realm of allegedly true and gentle feeling, however, was not in every woman's interest. Authors like Mary Wollstonecraft or Hedwig Dohm (to name but a few) felt offended by men's insistence on women's vulnerability and weakness and instead asserted their claim to personal honour, moral strength and intellectual wit.[186]

Second, such individual criticism often inspired collective movements. Around 1900, the youth movement set out to form and follow new emotional rules that strongly diverged from what they despised about bourgeois society. A few decades earlier, the women's movement had started to question opinions and practices that excluded women from well-esteemed professions and spheres of activity. In the 1960s, students launched a radical critique of "authoritarianism" in families, universities, and politics. They not only discussed academic texts, but also took their resentment and contempt to the streets, in a highly emotional and passionate way.

Third, even without those ferocious attacks, institutions were subject to change. Traditional family structures crumbled when more women got employed and earned their own money. The economic world underwent consecutive revolutions that increased the number of female employees as well as the weight of those sectors and branches that directly tended to clients and consumers. In their wake, so-called feminine qualities like empathy, care, and friendliness became ever more important. At the same time, institutions

like the military, which had traditionally been identified with male emotional dispositions like honour,
violence, and vigour, lost their appeal and power. Others, like schools or universities, opened themselves to
new subjects and modes of communication that were
less strictly and profoundly gendered. Politics, though
since the early twentieth century no longer off-limits
to women, largely kept its male attire both in content
and style. Compared to the 1830s when liberals had
commented on political passions going wild, sixty
years later the political mass market had turned into a
far more emotionalised arena. Post-World War I politics did nothing to attenuate emotions, rather the
contrary. Even the alleged return to sobriety after
1945 could not do without whipping up collective
worries, rage, and hatred as manifested in anti-Com-
munist or, in the case of France, anti-anti-colonialist
propaganda.[187]

As a fourth element of change, the impact that institutions and, for that matter, institutionalised norms
of emotional conduct bear on individuals has shifted
over time. On the one hand, more and more people
have been involved in the various institutions that
make up civil society. Schooling is a case in point.
Schools not only have become more inclusive in terms
of both social class and gender; they also keep their

students engaged for a much longer period of time. Their influence has thus risen considerably, while the army's has been reduced. In a similar vein, the labour market has reached out to a growing number of people formerly not exposed to its particular requirements and expectations.

Still, the amount of time spent in gainful employment has dropped, as working hours and the age of retirement have decreased. This has allowed for the expansion of free and leisure time which in turn has become commercialised and subject to what might be called a veritable industry of emotions. The world of entertainment, vacationing and, generally speaking, consumer culture has come to exert an ever firmer grip on the economy of emotions as practised in high capitalism. As much as it has added an emotional flavour to certain goods and services, it has helped to standardise feelings and emotional behaviour.[188]

Women here have been primary targets, but men have followed suit, in their own special ways. Since consumer items are often clearly gendered, so are the emotions attached to them. Nevertheless, gender differences seem to be becoming less explicit and far-reaching. Ads or movies increasingly show women succeeding in their profession and buying expensive gadgets. At the same time, men can express caring emotions towards their children and friends. The overall endorsement of emotions, firstly, by capitalist consumer culture and secondly, by the "triumph of the therapeutic," has quite evidently affected both genders.[189] In its turn, women's long-standing faculty to indulge in, reflect on, and talk about emotions has been re-evaluated. Men, too, are invited (and forced) to upgrade their emotional skills, become "emotionally intelligent" and literate, and try out new ways to communicate emotions. Schlegel's ideal of "independent femininity" and "softened masculinity" has gained momentum—without, however, completely erasing demarcation lines. Girls, indeed, no longer blush when greeted by male peers. But they still cultivate emotional styles and practices quite different to those of boys.

Chapter 3

Finding emotions

When reflecting on gender and emotions, finally and inevitably, empathy comes into mind. Women, as nineteenth and early twentieth-century authors seemed to believe, were particularly well equipped to feel what others felt. Their nature, the argument went, allowed them to be more "compassionate and benevolent" than men who often appeared "harsh and cold-hearted," more interested in their own well-being than that of others. Women's delicate bones, nerves, and blood vessels enabled them to sympathise with fellow beings, and closely attend to their weal and woe. In contrast, men were more capable of taking care of general issues and developing a public spirit considered the root of civic virtue and patriotism.[190]

Empathy, sympathy, compassion for women, public spirit and civic virtues for men: is this how the moderns ordered and gendered civil society's emotional resources and moral foundations? Or were there other ways of aligning feelings and actions, collective and individual passions? How and why did empathy matter at all to a modern society praising self-love, individual interest and personal achievement over the common good? What was considered good about sharing other people's emotions? And what kind of behaviour should this sharing generate?

Empathy and compassion

Present-day psychologists and neuroscientists lead us to distinguish between empathy, compassion and emotional contagion. The latter happens to babies who start crying when they hear other babies cry. They share their unpleasant feelings unknowingly. Only after human beings have learnt to differentiate between Me and You or Them, are they capable of empathy. They become aware that their emotional state is triggered by the emotional state of another person (or animal). Compassion in turn is defined as a pro-social emotion also invoked by another person. Feeling compassionate towards that person, however, does not imply feeling what the other one feels. Even if I do not experience the other's pain, I can still be committed to helping and improving their situation.[191]

The fact that neuroscience has recently focused on empathy as a preferred research topic is not surprising. Even before discovering the mirror neuron system that, through understanding other people's or animals' movements and intentions, navigates our own, emotions have been on the brain scientists' agenda. Other disciplines have followed and ennobled emotions as an academic topic. Evolutionary biologists seek to explain feelings of benevolence and altruistic behaviour as compatible with natural selection because they benefit the organism.[192] Economists were quick to seize upon this and, aided by neuroscientists, have modelled conditions under which altruism outperforms selfish attitudes.[193] Social scientists have become interested in the ways in which compassion is conveyed across borders and channelled into practical humanitarian work.[194]

Beyond academe, empathy and compassion hold their ground in numerous social practices and formats. People donate funds for those who have suffered from hurricanes, tsunamis, earthquakes or civil war. Compassion travels widely and connects Europeans with people living in faraway places. Being compassionate has become something like the gold standard of humanity, a moral quest which commands high authority and asks for immediate action. As such, it crept into the political programme of former US president George W. Bush who chose to speak of his government's "compassionate conservatism": "It is compassionate to actively help our citizens in need. It is conservative to insist on accountability and results."[195] More than a century earlier, Otto von Bismarck, first chancellor of Imperial Germany, had described his social policies as "practical Christianity." Social legislation, he argued, was to "ensure kindlier treatment" to the poor and keep alive their "sense of human dignity."[196]

Compassion, coupled with concepts of neighbourly love and human dignity, is thus obviously not a novel idea. It was already known and practiced, as Bismarck testifies, during the nineteenth century. It goes back, some argue, even further and seems as old as mankind. Eighteenth-century philosophers suggested sympathy and compassion to be natural human faculties which made them eternal and primordial. Medieval Christianity had praised *compassio* and *misericordia* as major virtues secondary only to the love of God. Those who were compassionate took other people's misery to heart and came to their rescue, out of love. Such attitudes and behaviour were considered good and rational, i.e., complying with *ratio humanae vitae*.[197] Other religions hold similar views. The Koran continuously refers to compassion and mercy (*rahma*) as major characteristics of God and as crucial virtues of the Islamic community.[198] Central to the Buddhist tradition are age-old meditative practices and techniques (*shamatha*) that focus on empathy. The person who meditates is advised to consider every human being as their teacher or mother, as someone very dear to them. This is supposed to enhance their compassionate perception and outlook.[199]

Social emotions in eighteenth-century moral philosophy

Training oneself to feel compassion, or bowing to compassion as an authoritative virtue, though, was not on the mind of those who, in the eighteenth century, elevated it to a crucial component of "the common good and welfare." For British moral sense philosophers as well as for French proponents of sensibility, pity and compassion were taken for granted. In 1728, Francis Hutcheson extolled them as "publick" affections about "the State of others." They "extend to all perceptive Natures, when there is no real or imagined Opposition of Interest. We naturally *desire* the absent Happiness of others; *rejoice* in it when obtained, and *sorrow* for it when lost." David Hume's *Treatise of Hu-*

man Nature published in 1739-40 saw the "passion of pity" arising from the "general principle of sympathy." Rousseau, for his part, conceived of *pitié* as an immediate, genuine emotion, caused by the aversion to see others suffer.[200]

Sympathy, as an overarching concept, was the cornerstone of moral philosophy invented by the Scottish Enlightenment. It laid the groundwork for social communication and cohesion, and it promoted a common morality among members of a given society. How this should and could work was described in great detail and allegedly based on empirical evidence. Hume took great care to point out that his observations did not depend "on any hypothesis of philosophy" but referred to "plainest experience." The latter proved that "the passions and sentiments of others [...] appear at first in our mind as mere ideas, and are conceiv'd to belong to another person." The ideas are then "converted into the very impressions they represent." They acquire "such a degree of force and vivacity, as to become the very passion itself, and produce an equal emotion, as any original affection." The process of conversion thus "make[s] us enter into the sentiments of others."

What caused and supported this was "resemblance." Since all human beings resembled one another, both in the "fabric of the mind, as with that of the body," they could embrace the opinions and affections of others "with facility and pleasure." Increasing resemblance would engender increased sympathy. In this respect, similar "manners, or character, or country, or language" allowed for stronger sympathy. Conversely, the "great uniformity" of humours and ideas found among members "of the same nation" arose from sympathy rather than "from any influence of the soil and climate." Resemblance thus facilitated sympathy which in turn fostered social integration and moral consensus. Accordingly, "the sentiments of others have little influence when far remov'd from us." Contiguity was necessary to communicate them.[201]

While sympathy played *basso continuo* in Hume's famous treatise, it trumpeted Adam Smith's equally important *Theory of Moral Sentiments*. Published in 1759, its first chapter immediately got to the point "of sympathy." Chapter two went on to speak "of the Pleasure of mutual Sympathy." Even more explicitly and consistently than Hume, Smith introduced sympathy as a natural principle underlying and buttressing man's ability to be a moral person and live in harmony with others. Similarly to Hume, Smith stressed the importance of imagination: in order to sympathise, a person had to change places with the one who suffered or felt joy, disgust, wonder, fear. Only by putting himself in the shoes of the other could one conceive or "be affected by what he feels." What Smith called "fellow-feeling" enabled the person to "enter into the sentiments" of others and feel what they felt.

For spectators with "delicate fibres and a weak constitution of body"—women, above all—this kind of fellow-feeling apparently came easy. But even "men of the most robust make" could experience it, as proven by empirical observation. (Smith, too, put great emphasis on being an empiricist). This would work even better if the one, who, in the first place, felt a certain emotion, tuned down its expression to a degree that could be more readily consumed by others. Here, Smith introduced a new concept: reciprocity and self-inspection. *A* was called upon to see his passion with *B*'s eyes which immediately "abates the violence of what he [*A*] felt" before. Instead of overwhelming and overcharging *B* in his ability and willingness to sympathise, *A* thus brought down "his emotions to what the spectator [*B*] can go along with."

Self-love and sympathy

Smith was quick to point out the conditions that allowed for such delicate procedures of reciprocal perspective-taking: "society and conversation." In the presence and under the observation of peers, "men of the world" were prompted to abate their passions, restore "the mind to its tranquillity" and achieve the "equality of temper" rendering civil society a pleasant place. Sympathy thus worked both ways: it produced fellow-feelings like pity and compassion, but it also forced people to reflect on their own feelings and take a different viewpoint. According to Smith, the reciprocity of sympathy engendered two sets of virtues: "the soft, the gentle, the amiable virtues, the virtues of candid condescension and indulgent humanity" on the one hand, and "the great, the awful, and respectable, the virtues of self-denial, of self-government" on the other. Civil society needed both: indulgent humanity and "that command of the passions which subjects all the movements of our nature to what our own dignity and honour, and the propriety of our own conduct, require."[202]

Why did Smith and Hume put so much weight on those amiable virtues, and why did they highlight sympathy and fellow-feeling, in particular? Did this not run counter to modern society's basic rules that Smith himself spelt out so powerfully and lucidly only a few years later? To this very day, Adam Smith is predominantly known and remembered as the author of *The Wealth of Nations* which, published in 1776, laid the foundations of modern economic theory. At the onset of Britain's industrial revolution, Smith championed free market economies as beneficial both to a country's internal development and to global cooperation. These economies, he argued, relied heavily on people's self-interest and the liberty to pursue it, in cooperation with others. Though triggered and practiced through selfish motives, cooperation ultimately served the interest of all, advanced general well-being and increased the wealth of a nation (and, for that matter, of all nations).

Where was the place of sympathy in a model that praised and glorified self-interest? To recall Smith's famous passage: "It is not from the benevolence of the butcher, the brewer, or the baker that we expect our dinner, but from their regard to their own interest. We address ourselves, not to their humanity but to their self-love, and never talk to them of our own necessities but of their advantages."[203] Then how did Smith get from sympathy to self-interest and self-love, and vice versa? Do these concepts not contradict and mutually exclude each other? Not for Smith: self-love and self-interest, as he saw it, did not preclude pity and compassion at all, but rendered them possible.

Smith, like many others, drew on the modern concept of the individual that declared himself (it was always a "he," and never a "she" in those days) as the ultimate bearer of freedom and self-determination. Self-interest was his motivation, and his goal was self-realisation, the free and independent practice of talents and strengths. In order to achieve that goal, however, a man needed other men with whom he competed and collaborated in the common quest for self-perfection. Sympathy allowed him to engage in this social enterprise and imbue society with "moral sentiments" that guaranteed its stability and cohesion as much as they fostered individual happiness.

This approach rested on two major premises: first, on the acceptance that self-love was not in itself despicable. Instead, it was held to be a natural and necessary emotion promoting the survival and well-being of the individual. This marked a crucial departure from pre-modern, mainly Christian ideas that tended to devalue and criminalise self-love and self-interest as immoral, as a sin before God and people. During the eighteenth century, self-love acquired a noble, civilising role, as a legitimate and even desirable emotion that, under certain circumstances, could be beneficial for society as a whole.

This is where the second premise applied: self-love and self-interest had to be balanced in relation to other needs and necessities. They were to be controlled and restrained, at times, and had to be incited and enhanced, at others. This is exactly what happened in social communication, or, more specifically, in the market. Men, as Adam Smith observed, shared a "propensity to truck, barter, and exchange one thing for another."[204] Bartering and exchange made them highly dependent on each other. In fact, their mutual dependence did not stop on the level of goods; it went further in the realm of passions and emotional transactions.

Passions (recognised as major forces behind human motivation and action) both increased men's vulnerability and indentured them to others. At this point, sympathy entered the stage. While "the agreeable passions of love and joy" did not demand "auxiliary" assistance, "the bitter and painful emotions of grief and resentment" did. They "strongly require," so Smith contended, "the healing consolation of sympathy." The latter thus served the recipient, but it also added to the well-being of the giver who found pleasure in being able to sympathise.[205]

Suffering and pity

Although sympathy was by no means restricted to pity and compassion, it was particularly pressing in case of suffering. Those who grieved for the loss of a beloved person, or fumed with rage, were in dire need of someone who shared their sentiments and offered them practical assistance and words of comfort. Where the reciprocal process of perspective-taking worked, it helped them to calm down their strong and violent feelings. Even if it failed, sympathy did wonders, as captured in proverbial language: "Misery loves company," "a sorrow shared is a sorrow halved," "geteiltes Leid ist halbes Leid."

In many ways, Smith's argument was similar to how Rousseau, across the Channel, thought about pity and compassion. Writing in 1755, he regarded *pitié* as natural and universal: "it is the pure emotion of nature, prior to all kinds of reflection" and reason. As such, it was one of the two principles that guided the "operations of the human soul": men cannot see another human being (or animal) suffer. *Pitié* thus accompanied and restrained the second principle: the concern for one's own "welfare and preservation."[206]

For Rousseau as much as for Smith, self-love and compassion were "natural" capacities of each and every human being, and the two had to be brought into "agreement and combination." Here is where the differences began. Whereas Rousseau thought of civil society as a stage in human development that hampered man's natural inclination to be compassionate, Smith vigorously disagreed. For him, civil society and a free-market economy went hand-in-hand with all kinds of sympathy. What he called "fellow-feeling" referred to "any passion whatsoever" and was not limited, as with Rousseau, to the suffering of pain and death. So while Rousseau evoked the dream of a paradise lost, Smith envisaged the future (in the present) as a state that happily aligned the progressive, forward-pushing force of self-interest with the comforting, sideways-looking power of sympathy.

Writing at about the same time, albeit in different places, might (at least partly) explain the contrast of opinion. Rousseau attacked the political and social order that he saw reigning on the European continent: Absolutism and chasms of social inequality. Smith, in turn, lived in Britain where politics were less oppressive, society was more open and mobile, and capitalism was already on the way. Hence the future looked more promising than the past, whereas for Rousseau, the future (after the downfall of despotism) was about getting closer to the benign state of nature, abolishing the division of labour (which Smith considered to be the source of economic progress) and the institution of private property.

Fraternité and the French Revolution

Twelve years after Rousseau's death, the French Revolution did put an end to the authoritarian (if not despotic) *Ancien Régime*. It failed, however, to finish off what the philosopher had held responsible for the wretched state of society: property, division of labour, social inequality. Still, it popularised two important innovations that both Smith and Rousseau had on their minds: the idea of universal human rights and the concept of *fraternité*. Those concepts proved to be milestones in the development of a modern social and global order, and both relied heavily on what Smith and Hume had called sympathy.

At first sight, they seemed to have much in common with traditional Christian notions of brotherhood. *Fraternité*, as evoked by the revolutionaries, was reminiscent of the semantics of brotherly love and the love of neighbour. Since early Christianity, following the Jewish example, fellow believers had addressed each other as brothers, thereby stressing the bonds of mutual love which their shared faith had fostered between them. The Middle Ages saw the development of special *fraternitates* comprised of monks living in different monasteries but belonging to the same spiritual community. Their model inspired merchants

163

and craftsmen to establish similar *confraternitates* or guilds combining religious and secular purposes. It also inspired German peasants who in 1524-25 revolted against feudal privileges and despotism. They called each other "Christian brothers" and invited others to join their "Christian union and *Bruderschaft*." The latter was thus not, as with monks and burghers, confined to certain institutions, but moved beyond them.

In the eighteenth century, this movement gathered pace. Freemasons took the lead and established a cult of brotherhood that departed from earlier models and traditions in two important ways. First, it was profoundly secular. Masonic lodges were decidedly irreligious and open to men of different faiths. Catholics, Protestants and Jews could and did join them to experience a brotherhood that life outside the lodges denied them. Second, freemasonry's idea of brotherhood cut across social borders. It integrated men of different social backgrounds; more precisely, it bridged the gap between the aristocracy and members of the well-to-do and well-educated middle classes. In the intimacy of the lodge, protected by its aura of secrecy, they could indulge in rituals of community and communication that were impossible and inconceivable in wider society. What counted, was man in his natural goodness rather than birthright and social rank. By exclusively applying the "spirit level of nature," freemasons appreciated each other as brothers, no more and no less.[207]

But what about those who did not belong to the community of Masonic brothers? Were they not also brothers, if nature set the tone? In principle: yes. In practice: no. The principle was in the good hands of Friedrich Schiller who, in 1786, wrote the poem that became known worldwide after Ludwig van Beethoven set it to music in his Ninth symphony. Here, Schiller who sympathised with freemasonry praised joy as the unifying force that turned all men into brothers. Taken together with the poet's outspoken cosmopolitanism, this was a clear commitment to brotherhood and brotherly love encompassing all humankind. In real life, though, things looked somewhat different. The Masonic lodges practiced brotherhood only amongst their own members, and Europe was far from being a peaceful, harmonious "family." Instead of the cosmopolitan ties that should connect "all intelligent people," "antagonistic egoism" defined the relations between states and nations. As much as Schiller wanted to believe in the telos of history precipitating "our humane century," it required more than healthy optimism to see it coming.[208]

Six weeks after the young professor had delivered his inaugural lecture on universal history at Jena University, the Paris crowd destroyed the symbol of the *Ancien Régime*. Immediately, *fraternité* was presented as one out of three main principles informing the ambitious project of shaping a new society. While

Fig 9.
"Les Douceurs de la fraternité" (1794).

egalité and *liberté* set rather abstract goals, *fraternité* gained an immediate appeal. It acted as a peacemaker prompting citizens to realise liberty and equality among themselves. Its practices—embracing, taking oaths, declaring love—were meant to reaffirm the positive spirit of community unbound by revolutionary action. Those who convened at the Champ de Mars to celebrate the first anniversary of the Storming of the Bastille pledged to remain united *à tous les Français* by the indissoluble ties of *fraternité*. The new French nation born from the fire of revolution thus conceived of itself as a nation of brothers linked by brotherly love, care, and solidarity.[209] At the same time, it extended brotherhood beyond its geographical borders, with or without the consent of other nations. For those who refused to *fraterniser*, *fraternité* was introduced by military force.[210]

Similar to the British idea of sympathy, the French notion of revolutionary *fraternité* departed from earlier traditions, patterns and practices and opened a new chapter of thinking about compassion and brotherly love. What had distinguished sympathy from the Christian notion of *misericordia* was threefold: first, its secular character, second, its reciprocity, and third, its alleged naturalness. Being secular meant that sympathy was neither restricted to those sharing the same faith ("Christian brothers") nor imposed as a demand by one's faith. Reciprocity ruled out the distinction between the "active" person who offered compassion, and the "passive" recipient of that feeling. It put both on a par and allowed them to constantly change places, whereas the religious virtue of *compassio* had left the active/passive divide untouched. Furthermore, *compassio* was an abstract normative pledge caused by the love of God and mankind and expected from men rather than being naturally felt. In contrast, sympathy sprang from human nature, it was a genuine human trait and, as such, universally shared. All over the world, men felt it, regardless of faith, class, nation, or gender. Its universality enabled it to travel and connect people from faraway places. Instead of being reduced to the "love of thy neighbour" (*Nächstenliebe*) as preached by Christianity, sympathy could, and would, extend worldwide.

Human rights

Still, it was easier to experience and enact when the other was not too far away, as Hume had remarked. This held equally true for *fraternité*, as the French were soon to acknowledge. It also held true for the principle of human rights that the French Revolution borrowed from its American forerunner. In order to justify the American colonies breaking away from the British Empire, the 1776 Declaration of Independence had referred to the "self-evident" truths "that all men are created equal, that they are endowed by their Creator with certain unalienable Rights, that among these are Life, Liberty and the pursuit of Happiness." The 1789 French *Déclaration des Droits de l'Homme et du Citoyen* echoed those truths by first stating that "men are born and remain free and equal in rights" and second qualifying the latter as "liberty, property, security, and resistance to oppression." Although the Déclaration was bold and progressive, its omissions were obvious. Women immediately understood that they were collectively excluded, as were the slaves in French colonies. The "natural, unalienable and sacred rights of man" thus did not even pertain to all those who were living on French soil. Only he who was considered citoyen by virtue of his gender, legal status and nationality, could enjoy those rights—and the *fraternité* that active citizenship implied.

Nevertheless, the gospel spread fast and wide and it encouraged those excluded to press for inclusion. In 1791, the female activist Olympe de Gouges published a *Déclaration des Droits de la Femme et de la Citoyenne* (and was guillotined two years later); at the same time, slaves in San Domingo rebelled and finally earned individual freedom as well as national independence in 1804. The promise and vision that the French National Assembly had sent out in 1789 stayed alive, even if it proved hard to implement. It inspired the quest for emancipation brought forward by European Jews, it pushed the case of His Majesty's (George IV) Roman Catholic subjects, and it provided ammunition to women's movements.[211]

Those movements were initiated by social groups that felt deprived of the "rights of man." Picking up the new gospel, they argued and fought against all kinds of restraints and discriminations that prevented them from enjoying personal liberty, property, and security. Their success, though, depended on the support of others. Even if all Jews or Catholics or women had been united in their quest for inclusion, they would not have been able to enforce it against the will of the powerful. They needed, so to speak, their consent, or, to put it less strongly, their compliance. This is where sympathy (or fraternity) played a part.

Abolitionism and the change in sensibility

How this worked can be studied particularly well for those movements developing in support of people or beings who seemed to be excessively exposed to human injustice and oppression. Abolitionism provides a good example. Its roots date back to the late eighteenth century when the first anti-slavery groups formed, first in Philadelphia, and later in Britain. Strongly inspired by religious beliefs in human equality, Quakers and Evangelical Anglicans started to campaign for abolishing the slave trade. They organised mass petitions and successfully boycotted slave-grown products like sugar. After the British government had given in and made slave trade on British ships illegal, they went on to push for a "prompt extinction of British colonial slavery," mainly in the Caribbean. They spoke at lectures and meetings, they helped slaves to escape and gave them shelter. In 1832-33, 1.5 million Britons signed anti-slavery petitions submitted to the London parliament which eventually passed the Slavery Abolition Act. As of 1834, all slaves in the British Empire were emancipated.[212]

Abolitionism instigated the first mass movement in modern history engaging people of all classes, age, and

gender. Although it bore religious overtones, it spoke
to more secular-minded citizens as well and resonated
with a wide constituency. Its language was clearly in-

Fig 10.
Anti-slavery medallions (late 18th and probably 19th century).

formed by the mode of sensibility that had developed
since the 1740s. In its wake, the Cartesian *cogito ergo
sum* (I think, therefore I am) was supplemented by the
motto *Je sens donc je suis* (I feel, therefore I am).[213]
Ennobling feelings and sensations as means of perception and judgment caused a surge of cultural practices
and techniques favouring introspection and sublima-
tion.[214] How to feel and how to share one's feelings
with like-minded people became a major concern for
those men and women who claimed to be sensible and

compassionate. Sensibility, *sensibilité, Empfindsamkeit* generated a public craze that was equally relevant for Britain, North America, France and German-speaking Central Europe. Nurtured by popular novels, it spread into personal notebooks, diaries, and letters, media that were by no means confined to women and/ or adolescents. The culture of sensibility was originally embraced by men, too, as much as it reached out to people of different social backgrounds. Apart from the rising middle classes, it appealed to members of the aristocracy and gentry, even though—or rather because—it often involved criticism of the alleged lack of sincerity and authenticity within the noble circles.

By the end of the eighteenth century, the cult of true and deep feeling became increasingly contested by those who found it lacking in strength and activity. For Kant, "the ineffectual sharing of one's feelings in order to appear sympathetically in tune with the feelings of others" was unmanly. In order to be "effectual" and taken "to heart," sympathy had to acquire an energetic quality.[215] This is exactly what happened in the various reform movements springing up at around the same time, without, however, being noticed and appreciated by Kant and other castigators of weak, feminine sensibility. Their members and supporters indeed put feelings to action thus defying the man-of-feeling image as quoting poetry and shedding tears over the sad fate of a novel's hero or heroine.[216]

Although abolitionism was by far the most inclusive of those reform movements, there were many others that similarly built on men's and women's capacity and willingness to put themselves in the place of other, less fortunate beings. In 1774, for instance, High Sheriff John Howard provided testimony of the wretched situation of English prison inmates to the House of Commons that immediately passed legislation to improve it. Three years later, Howard published an account of his long-term investigations on the state of prisons in England, Wales and other European countries. It found an eager readership and put prison reform on the wider humanitarian agenda. Edmund Burke, the influential Whig politician and public orator, heralded Howard as an original reformer full of "genius" and "humanity," who was ready to "take the gauge and measure of misery, depression and contempt; to remember the forgotten, to attend to the neglected, to visit the forsaken."[217] A few years later, Elizabeth Fry took a special interest in female prisoners and helped to found an association actively campaigning to reform their conditions. This led, in 1821, to the creation of the British Ladies' Society for Promoting the Reformation of Female Prisoners which was among the first nationwide women's organisations in Britain. Elizabeth Fry then pioneered a training school for female nurses thus providing Florence Nightingale with a personal and institutional role model.[218]

Far from indulging in passive sympathy and silent contemplation, women, alongside men as well as on their own, spoke out and took action when affected by the misery of others. While such sentiments and affections might have been around in earlier times, the nineteenth century saw them gaining momentum and inspiring philanthropic and professional associations. Imbued with the spirit of reform and self-help, civil society encouraged citizens to take matters into their own hands and bring "progress" to those who seemed in dire need of it. The cult of sympathetic feeling fuelled social concern and generated movements that proved vital in introducing social change.

Sympathy, lexical

Rather than disappearing from the agenda of modern society, sympathy and compassion thus entered it on a new scale and with far greater urgency than before. This is reflected, among other forms, in encyclopaedias. By the mid-eighteenth century, sympathy had mainly been described as a physiological, cosmic or magical connection. Zedler's *Universal Lexicon* in 1744 defined it as a natural concept of "hidden correspondence of two entities," namely planets, plants, and animals.[219] Two decades later, the French *Encyclopédie* discussed the physiological proofs of sympathy, defined as "this communication that body parts have with one another, which keeps them in an inter-dependency, in one position, in a mutual suffering, and carries to one part the pain and diseases that afflict the other." Sympathy was solely about pathologies here, and only in passing did the author acknowledge that pleasant feelings could be communicated as well.[220] From then on, though, it gradually gained a more complex social and moral meaning. A century after Diderot and d'Alembert, Pierre Larousse's *Grand Dictionnaire Universel du XIX siècle* took it to be, above all, a "natural inclination to share feelings and impressions that others experience."[221] In a similar vein, the 1847 edition of the German *Brockhaus* placed the "psychic" dimension of *Sympathie* above physiology: *Mitempfindung* (empathy) was introduced as the "spontaneous imitation of somebody else's sentiment." By feeling "Mitfreude und Mitleid" (sympathetic joy and compassion), we participate in this sentiment "as if we felt it ourselves."[222] This definition remained basically the same until today.

Furthermore, lexica mirror the growing moral importance of sympathy/empathy, and compassion. As early as 1739, Zedler declared that *Mitleidigkeit* (compassion) could very well co-exist with "rational self-love." He also stated that compassion was to have an active component. Rather than just contemplating and feeling sorry for the calamities that befell a friend, "reasonable compassion" should strive to restore the "good spirit and pleasure of the one who suffers."[223] Zedler here anticipated what intellectuals disliked about the "sensibility craze" by the end of the eighteenth century. As late as 1932, the difference between true and "false" compassion was evoked; "moral value" was only granted when compassion elicited help—which, in 2006, was further specified as "active help, lenience, and deference."[224]

So it was not enough just to feel what the other felt. This is what we nowadays call empathy—a word that entered the lexicon only a few decades ago. Since then, Anglo-Saxon philosophy and psychology have switched from the notion of sympathy to the concept of empathy. Yet, it is not always clear what the distinction really is about, and often the terms are used interchangeably.[225] For the sake of clarity, it makes sense to reserve empathy for what *Einfühlung* means in German. *Einfühlung* became prominent in psychology and aesthetic theory in the early twentieth century. It meant, by and large, that we can only know about our fellow human beings by entering their emotional state. By sharing their position and expressions, we yield sentiments in ourselves that we might project back onto them. Empathy in this sense does not involve, let alone require, any positive regard of the other.[226] In contrast, sympathy, as it has been used since the eighteenth century, couples empathy with a pro-social, cooperative and benevolent attitude towards the other person.[227]

Schopenhauer's Nächstenliebe *versus* *Nietzsche's* Fernsten-Liebe

Empathy, then, serves as the basis for emotions like sympathy or compassion to arise. But unlike empathy, sympathy and, even more so, compassion, has a goal: to intervene and to help. It is exactly this goal-orientation that became so prominent during the nineteenth century. Growing numbers of people started to turn compassionate feelings into active social service. They organised philanthropy on a large scale, they formed associations to reform social conditions, and they launched social movements to improve the lives of others and their own. German philosopher Arthur Schopenhauer mirrored this development when he, in 1839, declared compassion to be one of the three prime factors determining human behaviour (the other two being egotism and spite). Compassion, i.e., the direct, unmitigated concern for the suffering of another person, served as the true basis of morality, of justice and *Menschenliebe* or *caritas*. Schopenhauer called it a "mysterious" phenomenon since it escaped reason why one should completely identify with another person and, at least momentarily, lift the barrier between Me and You. Still, he found ample proof of it in everyday life: on a micro-social level, when a person gave his life for someone that he hardly knew; and on a grand scale, when Britain decided to abolish slavery, and the British government raised 20 million pounds to compensate registered slave owners. He also mentioned various initiatives to protect animals from human cruelty which had first been organised in Britain and, from the 1850s, had spread to Germany as well.[228]

Even though Schopenhauer did not succeed in winning the prize of the Royal Danish Academy of Sciences, to which he had submitted his reflections on "moral foundations," his argument, largely borrowed from Rousseau, proved very influential. It coincided with the *Zeitgeist*, both in stressing active deeds and in its claim to make the world a better place. Furthermore it tried, just as Rousseau had, to locate compassion (and morality) in human nature rather than in religious norms. Far more radically than Rousseau, Schopenhauer denied the authority of Christianity on notions of charity and benevolence. Religion, he argued, had relatively little impact on morality.[229] Instead, the latter derived from human nature itself, which was, by definition, universal and timeless.

Some decades later, Friedrich Nietzsche ferociously attacked what had developed into a secular, as he saw it, "religion of compassion." The democratic age had dictatorially put compassion—"down to the animal, up to God"—on the public and political agenda. It had institutionalised a morality of general compassion, a "mortal hatred" against suffering and an "almost feminine incapability" to watch living beings suffer. While European societies apparently considered this to be the climax and epitome of human civilisation, Nietzsche took his distance. He thoroughly despised what he called the "morality of gregarious animals," and identified compassion as the greatest threat to the "new" morality he envisaged for a post-democratic age of noble heroism[230].

Leaving those visions aside (though they appealed to many contemporaries), we may nevertheless find some important truths in Nietzsche's reflections and observations. Writing in the 1880s, the philosopher was witnessing (and rebelling against) a powerful contemporary trend of compassionate behaviour. Calling it weak and feminine brought to the fore his own fantasies of masculine strength and dominant morality. At the same time, Nietzsche clairvoyantly emphasised features of compassion that had escaped "old" moralists like Schopenhauer. First, he pointed to the (conscious or unconscious) intentions of those who inflicted "pain" on others by their own weakness and suffering. The "thirst to be pitied" was nothing but taking pleasure in one's own ability to exert power over others. Second, Nietzsche offered crucial insights into the psychology of benevolence. Feeling and acting pity was even more closely connected to power than asking for pity. Those who sacrificed life and limb did so because they desired power or wanted to sustain it. Everybody who suffered was a delightful gift for people neither proud nor noble but content with what normal, mediocre life had to offer. In this vein, "compassion is generally praised as the virtue of prostitutes." It appealed to those who were not strong and courageous enough to go "their own way" but depended on the love and gratitude of others. Third, their compassion actually shamed the person who received it, by violating their pride. Shaming, though, was tantamount to poor morality; conversely, the most humane behaviour was about sparing somebody shame.[231]

Instead of immersing oneself in shameful and emasculating *Nächstenliebe*, Nietzsche promulgated *Fernsten-Liebe*, i.e., love for those who were far away and not easily accessible. *Fernsten-Liebe*, he argued, escaped both the pitfalls of projecting love that one did not feel for oneself onto one's neighbour, and the perils of exclusion. "Those further away have to pay the price of your neighbourly love. When five of you are together, a sixth has to die."[232]

Compassion and its shortcomings

Highlighting the exclusionary power of charity and brotherly/neighbourly love, Nietzsche struck the right chord. More than a century earlier, the philosopher Moses Mendelssohn had made a similar argument. Translating Rousseau's Discours on human inequality into German, he critically engaged with his arguments on nature, civil society and compassion. The notion that men were originally inclined, as Rousseau believed, to feel pity did not seem convincing to Mendelssohn. Men took pleasure in "harmony and order," in perfection. So they were in pain when they encountered deficiencies and privation, and felt an urge to make things better. This is what Mendelssohn called *Mitleiden*, compassion. At the same time, he was well aware of compassion's condescending quality. A person who pitied another person was usually closer to *perfectibilité* and wanted the other to move up as well. Even Rousseau's natural *pitié* thus imposed a hierarchical relationship, an asymmetry between those who offered it and those who received it.

Mendelssohn, a tolerated Jew in Prussia, did not strive for pity. Pity merely left him at the hands of superiors who looked down on him and whose benevolence reminded him of his own shameful inferiority. What he chose instead and what really mattered to him, was love: love of the fellow human being who reflected God's own perfectibility. Love drove man to seek the company of others, enjoy their virtues, and perform the never-ending work of perfecting.[233] Hence, love was far more symmetric and reciprocal than compassion. While love formed bonds of equality, compassion presupposed the one who was compassionate to be better off and more well-equipped to help than the one on the receiving end. This was something that Mendelssohn, who could have easily put himself into the bottom position, was extremely sensitive about. Opting for love and sociability (*Geselligkeit*) instead of pity and nature seemed to offer more secure prospects for the member of a minority facing constant threats of discrimination, expropriation, and expulsion.

Apart from being asymmetrical and potentially condescending, pity and compassion proved to be emotions hard to share among people who had few things in common or did not even know each other. Hume had already remarked on how important contiguity was for sympathy to arise. Mendelssohn's dear friend Gotthold Ephraim Lessing, who, in Rousseau's wake, considered compassion to be the highest virtue, was equally aware that it was far easier to be evoked for people who were just like us and with whom we could easily identify. Sameness (resemblance, for Hume) and closeness helped, since very few people seemed morally prepared and able to identify with just anyone on grounds of bare humanity. Even if, as the *encyclopédistes* had claimed, sensibility was "la mère de l'humanité," fellow-feeling appeared to be much less in supply in real life than philosophers might imagine.[234]

Counter-forces and blockades

In fact, there were multiple causes that blocked sympathy, pity, and compassion. In addition to spatial distance and sheer ignorance, moral opinions and prejudices maintained their ground. The fashionable idea of cosmopolitanism and universal brotherly love exposed among others by Schiller, encountered strong opposition by those who championed the new concept of nationhood. *Fraternité*, as defined during the French Revolution, was first and foremost concerned with binding French citizens together. Patriotism, the love of fatherland and nation, worked in similar ways, often at the expense of internal and external enemies. Anthropologists attempting to classify the populations of the world increasingly dismissed Johann Gottfried Herder's positive appreciation of different cultures and people. According to Herder, all cultures counted as equal and should be valued in their own right. To those who disagreed, some people seemed to be more animal-like than others, which justified the former's repression and the latter's dominance. In the course of the nineteenth century, inferiority and superiority became more and more racialised, putting enlightened ideas of progress and development to rest. Inferior races, in this logic, were never to reach the stage and position that superior races had attained. Though their lot could doubtlessly be improved, they would always lag behind.[235]

This kind of structural depravity made it extremely difficult to embrace them with sympathy and brotherly love which, as Schiller had known only too well, presupposed basic equality. Instead, it turned them into objects of pity associated with asymmetry, hierarchy, and condescension. When European missionaries, administrators and educators embarked on their "civilising mission" in Africa and Asia, they were convinced that the colonial subjects were to benefit from their work. Exposing them to the "manly" compassion that went along with active and energetic assistance would eventually liberate indigenous people from traditional prejudice and primitive customs—without, however, completely eradicating racial difference and inequality. At the same time, it reinforced the Europeans' sense of superiority and empowerment. Compassion should, as Nietzsche observed, endear that power to the powerless and be returned by love and gratitude. If it failed to do so, as in the Indian uprising of 1857, the powerful resorted to other means.[236]

Those other means, namely unrestrained violence and repression, were ubiquitous when and where Europeans (and non-Europeans) went on a colonising mission devoid of any civilising purpose. When Himmler in 1943 explained to his SS officers why they had to slaughter Slavs and Jews, he deliberately dismissed and mocked Herder's notion of cultural equality ("written down in inebriation"). He called Russians, Poles, and Jews not just inferior, but subhuman races that had to be either enslaved or annihilated. Extending German decency (*Anständigkeit*), good nature and *Gemüt* (soul) to these foreign, non-Germanic people was utterly wrong and dangerous. Honesty, decency, loyalty and comradeship exclusively applied to "members of our own blood." It was only they who deserved the SS man's unconditional love, sacrifice, and sympathy.[237] Two years earlier, Hans Frank, General Governor of occupied Poland, had likewise requested his staff: "steel yourselves against any compassionate considerations." Compassion should "principally be reserved" for German people. Jews were simply to "disappear," and no German should, as some obviously did, criticise this as "cruel" and "harsh."[238]

In this case, sympathy and compassion were blocked by depriving others of basic humanity. As subhuman races, beasts and bacilli, Jews and Slavs were not deemed worthy of human sentiment and sensibility. Since they were depicted as genuinely bad, treacherous, and dangerous, they had actually earned harsh treatment. The propaganda strategy was built on the long-standing opinion that only good and innocent people befallen by misery and hardship deserved compassion. In contrast, those whose sufferings were caused by their own misdemeanours could not lay claim to our pity. As early as 1798, this "general attitude" was rebuked by some writers, demanding pity, above all, for those who had incurred guilt due to their own "follies, vice and blame." A true *Menschenfreund* and philanthropist owed compassion to every human being regardless of the other's character and conduct.[239]

Such generosity, however, was not particularly widespread among contemporaries. To pity a criminal who had brought misery to others and in return suffered punishment and humiliation, seemed very far from reality. As late as the 1860s, executions in Britain usually drew huge crowds rejoicing in "brutal curiosity," as the journalist and writer William Thackeray reported in 1840. Shameful sanctions like the garrote in France or Germany found approval among urban spectators, instead of provoking "feelings of charity and pity."[240] What moved bystanders to attend public spectacles of humiliation and punishment became a hotly debated topic. Kant and others admitted that "it is not exactly the nicest observation about human beings that their enjoyment increases through comparison with others' pain." At the very moment when they spontaneously rushed to help someone, they were "happy not to be entwined in the same fate. This

FRANÇOIS, PIERRE BILLARD
Condamné au Carcan.Par.Arret.du Parlement
le 18 février 1772.et banni à perpétuité

Fig 11.
Print "François Pierre Billard condamné au Carcan par arret du Parlement le 18 février 1772 et banni à perpétuité" (ca. 1771-1774)

189

is why people run with great desire, as to a theatre play, to watch a criminal being taken to the gallows and executed. For the emotions and feelings which are expressed in his face and in his bearings have a sympathetic effect on the spectators and, after the anxiety the spectators suffer through the power of the imagination (whose strength is increased even further by means of the ceremony), the emotions and feelings leave the spectators with a mild but nevertheless genuine feeling of relaxation, which makes their subsequent enjoyment of life all the more tangible."[241]

In present-day language, it would have been empathy leading spectators to experience the shame and anxiety of the person humiliated and executed. Empathy is, so to speak, value-neutral. It is not always accompanied by feelings of deep sorrow, nor does it necessarily trigger emotions like revenge and gratification. More often than not, empathy involves the thrill of knowing for sure that one's own fate is different from (and better than) that of the person observed from a position of relative security and well-being. Fellow-feeling in this and related cases (like watching horror movies or documentaries of real atrocities today) goes hand in hand with the certitude that we are just onlookers and are spared the fate of the person(s) concerned. As much as people experience anguish, anxiety and disgust at the sight of those who suffer, they also feel pleasantly "relaxed" in the Kantian sense since they are not directly involved.

In order to turn this kind of empathy and "pleasant sadness" into active, engaging sympathy or compassion, or into equally active resentment or satisfaction, another trigger was needed. It depended heavily on how the event was framed: on its "ceremonial" and ritualistic character, on what was known about the person who suffered, and about the reason why he/she suffered, on the social and cultural proximity between them and the spectators, as well as how the spectators conceived of the legitimate or illegitimate power of those who inflicted this suffering.

Suffering, pity, and the education of feelings

Suffering as such, as Nietzsche observed, subsequently became a problem for modern morality. While the philosopher considered it a *sine qua non* for elevating man to greatness, high spirit, and arcanum, "the world" of "modern ideas" strove to abolish suffering altogether.[242] Philanthropic and reform movements sought to eradicate grief and misery from human life and experience rather than contenting themselves with alleviating and soothing suffering, as religion had tried for ages.[243] The ban on torture and slavery, the ongoing debate about the wrongs of corporal punishment in schools, prisons, and armies, the campaign against public executions and humiliating practices like floggings or running the gauntlet were all targeted by those who put empathy to the active test of civil society. Corporal punishment not only inflicted pain, it also humbled and degraded a person in the eyes of others. In addition, it took away one's sense of honour and self-esteem and debased, as Prussian legal reformers warned in the 1790s, "morality" and the "character of the nation."[244]

Instead, the latter had to be cultivated as much as possible and lifted to civilised standards. Although the state could not directly govern and regulate the citizens' hearts and minds, it could at least discourage them from behaving in ways deemed morally dubious and socially dangerous. And it could, in its own right, abstain from legal practices that evidently hurt public and private morality. Putting criminals in yokes, for example, was a measure reproved by *l'humanité*, as the French public prosecutor and *chevalier* of the *Légion d'Honneur*, Alexandre de Molènes, wrote in 1830. But it was not just the criminals' humanity that was violated by such a shameful sanction. The humanity of those who watched the spectacle was equally at stake. As Molènes and others criticised, the public, state-sanctioned display of cruelty conditioned the audience to "tread pity underfoot," defy shame and "forget all sentiments of human dignity."[254] Those who came to watch the dreadful procedure in great numbers, obviously indulged in the sight of someone being rightfully punished and humiliated. This seemed increasingly unacceptable as it nourished *Schadenfreude* instead of compassion and civil conduct.

So, even if it were a natural sentiment, as British, French and German philosophers claimed, compassion definitely needed to be enhanced and cultivated. Just like other feelings, it depended on education and refinement. Rousseau singing the gospel of pure nature, nevertheless acknowledged that "temperaments," allowing feelings to flourish or not, varied greatly according to the manner in which a person had been raised. He also admitted that moral sentiments like love were *"factice né de l'usage de la société."*[246] In a similar vein, Adam Smith championed a moral economy of emotions carefully calibrated and fine-tuned to the needs of civil society. Passions, affects, and appetites had to be "dignified" and had to undergo constant "recollection and self-command." This was not just about repressing or containing emotions or "bringing them down" to moderate standards so that "others can enter into" them. It was also about nurturing emotions held to be indispensable and socially desirable. As much as outright fury and anger were considered despicable, the lack of indignation in cases of grave injury appeared equally "contemptible." A person "who tamely sits still and submits to insults" did not receive sympathy, but was required to show some resentment if he wished to gain his peers' approval and support.[247]

Upon closer examination, then, there is nothing "natural" about emotions, not even about sympathy and compassion. The very moment a human being comes into the world, emotions start getting taught, trained, and economised to suit society's cultural framing. From early childhood, display rules become communicated and practised so that, as Nietzsche lucidly observed, they influence what is felt and how it is felt. Even if those rules merely aim at moderating the passion's "language and gestures," they eventually change the passion proper.[248]

Modern dilemmas

Within the greater picture of the modern economy of emotions, compassion evidently occupies an important place. Moral and social reformers in Europe turned it into a cornerstone of civil sensibilities, and introduced various practices and regulations to feed and sustain it. Building on older notions of Christian love and benevolence, they strove to secularise compassion both as a so-called natural sentiment *and* a responsibility shared by all citizens. They founded philanthropic and humanitarian associations, promoting compassion on a large scale. They turned to the public, canvassing for support by appealing to the "fellow-feeling" of fellow-citizens. In this vein, compassion became what sociologist Niklas Luhmann called a communicative or symbolic code allowing and encouraging people to form and express appropriate feelings.[249]

That code, however, did not always encounter approval. Although compassion had been "invented" as a truly democratic emotion based on the equality of mankind, this was soon questioned and refuted. Many a social movement that sprang up during the nineteenth century did not demand compassion, but justice. Rather than drawing on the compassionate support of others, its members were eager to rely on, and help themselves. In such a context, sympathy and compassion lost their inclusive meaning and were limited exclusively to those who shared common interests, desires, and needs. The labour movement, for instance, reserved sympathy only for workers who had formed bonds of fraternity and solidarity among each other. They felt no sympathy for the capitalist entrepreneur, and they did not expect his sympathy. Class society and class struggle more or less caused the concept of general and universal sympathy and compassion to collapse. Practices of self-help, *mutualité*, and solidarity among workers of similar backgrounds turned out to be far more important than the philanthropic services of middle-class men and women.

Eventually and ever more so, it became obvious that empathy, sympathy, compassion, and pity were burdened by a structural dilemma. On the one hand, modernity took them to be natural, universal, and democratic emotions supposed to unite people regardless of their social and ethnic status. This was the line of thought that informed the American Declaration of Independence and the French Declaration of the Rights of Man and Citizen and, in their wake, the Universal Declaration of Human Rights adopted by the General Assembly of the United Nations in 1948.[250] It also informed those social movements that pressed for the abolition of slavery, torture, and shame sanctions. Furthermore, it was the driving force behind associations aiming to prevent cruelty against animals or children.

On the other hand, the argument that sympathy was natural and universal was riddled with serious flaws. If it rested, as Smith, Rousseau or Schopenhauer claimed, on a person's imagination of what others might feel, it was logically restricted to one's own universe of feelings. Strictly speaking, imagination works in two steps: first, the person imagines how they would feel in a given situation (say, under torture or in slavery), and second, they imagine the other to feel just like they would. The problem here is that we can imagine certain situations better than others. This is why we feel socially inclined to sympathise more with those people with whom we can identify, than with others who live in different worlds. Even if we managed to identify with the latter, we would presumably get it wrong, and our compassion would be misled. To give an example: a non-Muslim Western woman might feel awkward seeing a Muslim woman wearing a hijab and putting herself in the other's shoes—but does this allow her to assume that the Muslim woman has the same feelings?

This is where we encounter the limits of empathy, sympathy and compassion as epistemological and political caveats. Those limits not only pose the question on what grounds we can identify with, and feel compassion for, strangers; they also challenge us to find practical ways of acting compassionately beyond the borders of our small worlds. Modernity has solved the first problem by declaring compassion a social norm that rests on the assumption of universal human rights as they were postulated in 1776, 1789 and, above all, in 1948. In order to be put into practice, though, these universal rights need to draw upon real people's sympathy and compassion. Despite philosophers' claim to the contrary, fellow-feelings do not come naturally. Even if, as neuroscientists try to demonstrate, empathy is a universal feature of human beings, it has to be translated into pro-social behaviour. Culture and social practices are of vital importance when it comes to feeling compassion towards strangers, acting compassionately and energetically protecting human dignity. People need strong additional incentives to do what nature allows them to do. They need supportive environments, both materially and in terms of values and ideas. They need role models, and they need the space to test and experiment with various forms of empathic action.

Historically, Europeans have found different solutions to this puzzle. Firstly, they refused the general norm and avoided its pressure by restricting compassion to well-defined groups only. This applied to charitable and philanthropic associations deliberately operating on a small scale. Taking care of the local poor, improving the condition of maltreated children or animals or collecting money for the victims of fire or flooding comforted the moral conscience of the middle classes and contributed to social harmony and stability. In their vast majority, those practices relied on interpersonal communication; the "objects" of compassion were known to those who acted in a compassionate way. Even if they were socially or ethnically different, they were no strangers: they belonged in the same town, region or nation.

When the idea of the nation as an "imagined community" (Benedict Anderson) gained political prominence during the nineteenth and twentieth centuries, nationalism tended to reserve compassion for members of the national community—and, potentially, for those who "fraternised" with that community. An extreme model of nationalist inclusion and exclusion came to the fore during the interwar period. In 1939, a German lexicon defined *Mitleid* (compassion) as "instinctive empathy" (*Miterleben*, *Mitfühlen*, *Sichhineinversetzenkönnen*) that was felt only toward *Gemeinschaftsgenossen*, i.e. toward those living in one's own community.[251] Those who lived outside this community or were expelled from it could neither hope for instinctive empathy nor expect distinctive compassion. Instead, they were exposed to unforeseen brutalities (which, then, triggered a new interest in human rights and led to the 1948 UN Declaration).

Secondly, modern societies witnessed another form of restricted or particular compassion: self-help movements relying on notions of in-group solidarity rather than asking for the compassion of others. Instead of feeling empathy for strangers of any kind, those movements limited compassion first and foremost to their own kind. Within capitalist democracies, this strategy helped them gain strength and bargaining power. At the same time, however, they tried to tear down nationalist barriers and demarcations. The labour movement as much as women's and peace movements deliberately reached out to like-minded people all over the world. They went global, in this sense, but not universal.

Humanitarianism and its crises

Thirdly, this was left to modern humanitarianism emerging in the late eighteenth century and gaining momentum mainly after WWI. It claimed to radically differ from former notions of charity and *misericordia* by being both universal and actively engaged in the aim to eradicate misery. Humanitarianism was highly interventionist and operated on a global scale. It no longer accepted the idea of the stranger, but propagated the concept of the brother (and later, the sister). The grounds on which brotherhood and sisterhood were offered—and, for that sake, traded—changed considerably over the course of time. Religious beliefs gradually lost importance and authority, in most parts of Europe. They were replaced by more secular notions of human rights that belonged to, and had to be defended by, everyone. Notwithstanding their secular character, however, those rights were declared "natural, inalienable *and sacred*" by the French National Assembly in 1789, testifying to the unabated relevance of religious language even among revolutionaries[252].

The first transnational humanitarian movements focused on the abolition of slavery, and they proved enormously influential. More followed soon: in 1863, Swiss businessman Henri Dunant founded the Red Cross which quickly became a truly international institution (and, approximately sixty years later, spurred the foundation of the Red Crescent). 1959 saw the birth of *Terre des Hommes* and its struggle against child labour, child prostitution and malnourishment.

Since 1971, *Médecins Sans Frontières* have been working in conflict areas and refugee camps offering basic health care. At about the same time, organisations like *Amnesty International* or *Human Rights Watch* were established, raising public awareness of human rights violations. What all these movements and organisations have in common is their impartiality and political neutrality: they do not take sides, but focus, instead, on trying to help victims regardless of their background.

With the citizens' willingness to donate money for its causes, humanitarianism has become a huge enterprise worth ten billion dollars every year, tendency rising. Private voluntary associations, UN offices, and national agencies are all active players in the global market of emergency relief and humanitarian assistance.[253] They seem to embody what the economist Amartya Sen has recently called, with reference to Adam Smith's "impartial spectator," the non-parochialism of distant, though empathic perspectives.[254] And they give credence to what others chose to call the "empathic civilisation" and its "race to global consciousness."[255]

Yet, this new secular religion has also got its dark sides. On the one hand, it is far less universally committed than claimed. Donating money, for instance, follows special trends and selection procedures which may be politically and culturally biased. When in January 2010 much of Haiti's infrastructure was destroyed by an earthquake killing and injuring more than half a million people and leaving another million homeless, money was donated to a far greater extent in comparison to Pakistan which experienced dramatic flooding later that year. This has been attributed, among other reasons, to Pakistan's negative image associated with terror, corruption and religious fanaticism. Media bear a huge impact on how such images are constructed, circulated and communicated. What they broadcast, and for how long, directly influences people's inclination to feel pity and responsibility. Exposure to dramatic pictures and messages motivates people to act in a more generous manner.

On the other hand, the media's influence is ambivalent, at best.[256] As much as global journalism seeks to generate empathy with distant suffering, it spreads pictures of violence that produce the opposite results: apart from inciting acts of imitation, these pictures have emotional side-effects hardly compatible with empathic, pro-social outlooks and behaviour. They may, as eighteenth-century philosophers argued, elicit many kinds of pleasure, including a sense of *Schadenfreude*. In an age before mass communication and ubiquitous visualisation, however, philosophers could not imagine that such pictures might eventually over-burden and exhaust empathy and compassion. They might even kindle a certain aversion to explicit moral claims to engage with the suffering of others, and lead, instead, to chagrin and withdrawal.[257]

Emotions lost and found:
Conclusions and perspectives

We have come to the end of our intellectual journey. It took us from the French president's anger to global empathy; it fathomed women's rage and allowed us to question men's cold blood; it introduced us to honour cultures and examined practices of social shaming. With regard to time, we travelled from the eighteenth to the twenty-first century, in some cases going even further back in time. Geographically, the journey started in the midst of Europe, in Brussels, from where we set off in different directions: mainly to France, Great Britain, and the German-speaking countries. On our way, we encountered Spanish *hombres de honor* and Sicilian *mafiosi*, met Algerian and Turkish immigrants, and briefly crossed the Balkan war theatre.

Omitting Northern and Eastern Europe altogether, due to lack of language skills and expertise, the book focused on Europe's western and central areas. Despite manifold national and regional differences, they share cultural traits and political institutions, commercial developments and social movements that proved pivotal for the way in which the economy of emotions was structured and evolved. Furthermore, throughout the modern period, those areas were closely interconnected, for better or worse. As much as people, goods, and news circulated more or less freely, emotional codes and styles informed and borrowed from each other, from the Age of Sensibility (succeeded by the Revolutionary and Napoleonic Wars) to the Age of the Therapeutic (preceded by the Second Thirty Years War).

Yet, these codes and styles did not apply to all people living in Western and Central Europe during the modern period. How men and women, adolescents and senior citizens, peasants and city dwellers dealt with their emotions, how they regulated, managed, navigated and reflected upon them, did not follow the same pattern. Immigrant communities harboured emotional regimes that frequently differed substantially from those of the host society, and were radicalised even further once those differences became judged as cultural markers on both sides. Within the host society, social subcultures, particularly in adolescence, constructed their own universe of feeling that often bore little resemblance to how other youth or adult groups set up their economy of emotions. To give a contemporary example: "Emos" have become a significant subculture within urban European youth culture in recent years. They deliberately set themselves apart from others by cultivating special dress codes, musical styles and emotional communication that sometimes verges on the auto-aggressive. Their outer appearance and behaviour have very little in common with self-assertive, abrasive youth gangs, and they do not match the culture of coolness as it pervades late modern Western mainstream society.[258]

Keeping this heterogeneity in mind, it is highly questionable to speak of emotional regimes, styles and codes *tout court* and imply that they pertain totally to social systems or national territories. Historically, we might be tempted to assume that late modern societies show less social and cultural diversity than early or premodern ones. Advanced consumer economies and all-pervasive media coverage seem to provide more homogeneous patterns of consumption, communication and appearances. The proliferation of self-help literature, for instance, addressing unisex and unisocial audiences, invites us to think that their advice and counsel is sought and followed by each and everyone. However, this is at best half-true. For a start, social norms and prescriptions as they are defined by the genre, do not always translate into practice, let alone produce uniform behaviour. Even if a message is not completely lost on readers (it rarely is), they might find it hard or unfeasible to follow the rules.

Furthermore, those rules and prescriptions as they are transmitted via media images and therapeutic handbooks are in no way unique, let alone only relevant to our times. In early modern Europe, religious texts like sermons, prayer books, and spiritual writings worked as powerful emotional educators conveying strong normative scripts. On more worldly matters, advice manuals began to get published by the end of the late eighteenth century and were circulated widely during the nineteenth and early twentieth centuries. In contrast to previous and present efforts, those books were more exclusive as they were written for, and directed at, segregated audiences: young versus adult men/women, rural versus urban, Catholic versus Protestant, rich versus poor. The general tone was set, however, by the educated upper (and) middle classes all over Europe who strove to claim and exert cultural hegemony.

This is also the reason why these social milieus have taken centre stage in this book. Focusing on European honour cultures, in the first chapter we explored some crucial features of their emotional self-perceptions and practices. In the second chapter, we tracked emotions invading gender roles and relations that were first and foremost spelt out for men and women of bourgeois family background. Finally, the third chapter acquainted us with modes of empathic and compassionate behaviour implemented by (mostly) middle-class members of social reform and humanitarian movements.

Again, this is not to suggest that those practices and self-perceptions dominated modern societies and eradicated social differences and diversity. In fact, as far as honour is concerned, the opposite seems to be true. Men who held on to highly emotionalised practices like duelling were but a tiny minority and they neither attempted nor managed to turn their passions into a general rule. Still, the honour culture as it was performed by social elites had a far greater impact on society than the habits of marginal or liminal groups. Even if the latter seem to follow similarly self-assertive and agonal scripts (by, for instance, claiming "respect" and addressing each other with sexually explicit language and gestures), they operate in a social and emotional environment that clearly limits and weakens their appeal and resonance.

What further distinguishes such subcultural practices from the elite culture is the latter's influence on social institutions. Even though "men of honour" did not predominate in numbers, they had a firm grip on institutions like the courts, universities or the army. As long as respective social practices and feelings were enshrined in professional codes of conduct, they enjoyed high social visibility and an aura of importance that lower classes or marginal styles could not even dream of attaining.

Institutions also played a part as essential amplifiers that helped to disseminate emotional norms and rules. It was one thing to write and publish religious texts, advice books or novels that informed readers about what to feel and how to express their feelings. Educational tools and mechanisms were needed in order for this information to capture people's imagination and translate into social practices. Institutions like family, church, school, the military, the workplace and politics served as "schools of emotions" that shaped the self-perception and outlook of generations of respective students.

This does not imply, however, that curricula remained invariant. Just as honour practices like duelling vanished from the twentieth-century military and academic agenda, pedagogical institutions came to reassess the role emotions played in teacher-student relations. Families negotiated and altered gendered practices of emotional investment, and today's business world values CEOs' emotional literacy. Yet, what emotional literacy (or intelligence) means varies considerably. Modern institutions did not and do not all follow the same emotional script; rather, they provide distinct, sometimes divergent, expectations and propositions. As individuals constantly rotate between institutions and switch from one code of conduct to the other on a daily basis or during the life course, they have to deal with numerous feeling and display rules. How to navigate between them and accommodate one's personal needs and tastes becomes a major challenge in multi-layered, globalised societies.

The book's focus was not so much how individuals cope with that challenge but rather how institutions frame their emotional provisions and requests. The latter reveals a lot about the role emotions play in modern societies, how they are valued and endorsed. It also sheds light on how they are defined, regulated, and monitored. It could be argued that emotions, above all social or "relational" emotions, are deeply cultural. Although clearly resting on a physiological basis grounded in human (and animal) biology, they acquire culturally specific forms and meanings.

Consider empathy, for instance. The fact that human beings are naturally equipped to feel what others feel does not mean that they always do. They might just turn away and act indifferent. Or they might choose to combine empathy with *Schadenfreude* when watching others suffer in pain (or they might feel jealous when seeing other people thrive). To transform empathy into pro-social emotions and behaviour, people seem to need incentives and encouragement. They depend on educational inputs and social institutions that reinforce and amplify moral claims to compassion. How far compassion reaches and where it ends is equally dependent upon social, cultural and political factors. There might be situations and circumstances which restrict compassion to small circles of like-minded peers. In other instances, people extend compassion to distant sufferers regardless of causes or qualities. In any case, compassion needs explicit translations between those who suffer, and the "sensibilities" of those who may organise support.[259] These mediations occur through culture, i.e. through public media, associations and movements activating traditions, aligning interests, and legitimising feelings and actions deemed appropriate.

Emotions are thus framed within an economy that depends on, and answers to, cultural expectations and social needs. They become nurtured and cultivated on certain occasions, or otherwise repressed and sanctioned They are subject to processes of education and formation which operate on an institutional as well as on a personal level. As a rule, emotions are inevitably personal and individual; a group, a community or an institution, for that matter, cannot by nature have emotions. But they can, and do, influence and coordinate how and what their members feel and how they may express their feelings. They can encourage and discourage them to feel shame, pride or honour; they can support them to show or withhold rage, hatred, and compassion.

They also have a say on how emotions are gendered and if (and to what extent) men or women are supposed to feel (and act) differently. As for empathy, women have long since been credited with a particular ability to feel with and for others. Nineteenth-century physicians, psychologists, and other learned men believed that a "special anthropology" applied to women, which rendered them capable of effortlessly sharing other beings' sentiments and ailments. Emotions became naturalised in a way that had a crucial bearing on modern ideas and practices of empathic conduct. On the one hand, this allowed women to play a major role in associations and movements concerned with philanthropy and social reform. This was an important step at a time of hard efforts to confine women to the private sphere of family and friendship. More and more middle-class women took this step thus entering the public sphere and working side by side with husbands, brothers or cousins for the improvement of social welfare.

On the other hand, empathy was not held to be women's monopoly. As much as sympathy and compassion were seen as essential resources of modern society, all citizens had to embrace it and to develop attitudes beyond self-love and self-interest. Men's social status depended on their faculty to sympathise with others, and so did their ability to interact and cooperate in the fields of work and politics. According to public opinion, however, men's inclination to feel and enact sympathy differed from women's in an important way: it was far more pro-active. Even if women allegedly harboured more intense and gentle feelings, they were not thought to be able to turn them into appropriate behaviour due to physical and moral weakness. Men, in contrast, were deemed strong enough to let actions follow sentiment.

This was what and how numerous contemporaries thought and felt about the gendered economy of emotions. Their ideas were not just personal beliefs, but social scripts embedded in institutions like family, school, university, professional associations and organisations. They translated into feeling and display rules confronting men and women with strong expectations and sanctions. Yet, those expectations were not set in stone. They could be reviewed and negotiated, as it happened in social reform movements like abolitionism, engaging both genders and letting women take an active stance as much as men did. They could be questioned, criticised, rejected, and subverted by individual men and women who might become role models for larger groups and movements. Emotional norms, just as any social norm, were always in flux inviting individual agency as well as collective bargaining.

How this has worked throughout history is a fascinating research topic. Recently it reappeared in historiography and social science, which, after an early and short-lived phase of academic interest, had dismissed emotions as trivial and without explanatory value. "New" cultural history and sociology have taken them on board stressing their relevance for economic development, political communication, and social relations as well as for the construction and framing of subjectivity. Modern societies have come up with economies of emotions that match institutional arrangements and personal identities, buttress certain forms of social interaction and delegitimise other ones. To "find" emotions in history means to pay tribute to those economies and reconsider their impact on social and political conflict, cohesion and development, as well as on individual self-concepts and behaviour.

"Finding emotions" also means exploring the dynamics and trajectories that allow for some emotions, like honour and shame, to get lost and other ones, like empathy and compassion, to gain momentum during the modern period. The concept of "lost" emotions is somewhat problematic, though. According to the physicists' laws of conservation, nothing is ever lost in history. Cultural memory allows us to store ideas and concepts that have lost their practical appeal, and enables them to reappear in different forms, guises and meanings. In the case of *acedia*, melancholy and depression discussed in the first chapter, feelings of laziness, sloth and inertia might have travelled across cultures and periods. It is difficult to draw a strict line between *acedia* and melancholy, or between melancholy and depression, since they all share certain features. However, the language and manner in which they were framed varied greatly, and they applied to particular groups with very little in common. They were also explained and treated differently—which suggests that the way in which laziness, sloth and inertia have actually been felt and experienced by distinct groups and generations has changed considerably.

As for honour and shame, the case is slightly different. Given that the words are still in use, we might think that we know what honour and shame felt like one or two hundred years ago. But history proves us wrong. Just as the actress Hanna Schygulla could not understand and empathise with Effi Briest's feelings of shame, male middle-class Europeans nowadays will find it hard to enter Baron von Innstetten's feelings when learning of his wife's infidelity. Today's husbands would probably experience fits of jealousy and anger at having been deceived; they would not, however, feel insulted in their personal honour and they would not call out the person who had insulted them.

In sociological terms, this can be attributed to honour losing its grip in and on modern society in the course of democratisation and increasing plurality. Honour usually works successfully with segregated groups and circles that want to remain apart from others and cultivate distinct emotional styles. As long as those groups remain marginal and liminal, they can do this without challenging civil society's overall values and commitments. As a privilege of elite groups claiming social superiority, however, honour could not survive since it radically challenged and undermined the pluralistic, anti-hierarchical fabric of democratic systems.

Hence, we can argue that the emotional or "internal" disposition of honour was lost, it became obsolete, and was succeeded by both a general sense of human dignity and a meritocratic notion of "external" honour(s). Modern society thus worked to continuously shift and redress the range and rules of its emotional economy, discarding some passions and inciting others. The latter held true for empathy and compassion. Although pity and compassion had been present in premodern times, they have been substantially reframed and have gained new momentum since the eighteenth century. In this book, they therefore figure as "found" emotions: they were found to be crucial and indispensible for modern society, they found theoretical attention and acclaim as well as practical encouragement and institutional support. As social emotions, they conspicuously entered the public arena, while honour faded into the background. But as much as they promised a new utopia of universal humanity, they encountered real-life obstacles, structural dilemmas and blockades.

Exploring those counter-forces helps us to understand how emotions are embedded into social and cultural environments, how they are stirred, mobilised and silenced. This is as much a historical question, as it is one that concerns us as citizens. "Empathy," in the words of Piotr Cywiński, the current director of the Auschwitz-Birkenau State Museum in Poland, "is noble." But "it is not enough to cry" over past suffering. Instead, we should feel a "responsibility to the present."[260] The history of emotions informs us how to handle such responsibility and what to avoid along its path.

Notes

1   http://www.ft.com/cms/s/0/7ded6ae6-c1b9-11df-9d90-00144feab49a.html#ixzz163bayNzr; http://www.guardian.co.uk/world/2010/sep/16/nicolas-sarkozy-keeps-dismantling-roma-camps; http://www.channel4.com/news/articles/politics/international_politics/sarkozy%2Broma%2Bcomments%2Bapo soutrageousapos/3768007.html (last access: Nov. 23, 2010). All translations from German and French, if not otherwise noted, are mine.
2   Klein, Donald C., "The Humiliation Dynamic: an Overview," *Journal of Primary Prevention* 12, no. 2 (Dec. 1991): pp. 93–121, quote p. 97; Miller, William Ian, *Humiliation and Other Essays on Honor, Social Discomfort, and Violence* (Ithaca: Cornell University Press, 1993), ch. 4; Lindner, Evelin, *Making Enemies: Humiliation and International Conflict* (London: Praeger Security International, 2006).
3   *Frankfurter Allgemeine Zeitung*, May 13, 2009 (quoting chief rabbi Meir Lau and public intellectual Tom Segev).
4   As to the link between consumer marketing and emotions, see Illouz, Eva, *Consuming the Romantic Utopia: Love and the Cultural Contradictions of Capitalism* (Berkeley: University of California Press, 1997); eadem, *Cold Intimacies: The Making of Emotional Capitalism* (Cambridge: Polity Press, 2007).
5   Trentmann, Frank, ed., *The Making of the Consumer: Knowledge, Power and Identity in the Modern World* (Oxford: Berg, 2006).
6   Barker-Benfield, Graham J., *The Culture of Sensibility: Sex and Society in Eighteenth-Century Britain* (Chicago: University of Chicago Press, 1992), ch. 4, esp. pp. 211–14; Brewer, John and Roy Porter, eds., *Consumption and the World of Goods* (London: Routledge, 1993); Bermingham, Ann and John Brewer, eds., *The Consumption of Culture 1600–1800: Image, Object, Text* (London: Routledge, 1995).
7   Hutcheson, Francis, *An Essay on the Nature and Conduct of the Passions and Affections, with Illustrations on the Moral Sense*, ed. Aaron Garrett (Indianapolis: Liberty Fund, 2002), p. 47.

[8] Berger, Peter, "On the Obsolescence of the Concept of Honor," in *The Homeless Mind*, eds. Peter Berger et al. (New York: Random House, 1973), pp. 83–96.

[9] *Frankfurter Allgemeine Zeitung*, July 13, 1974, p. 19.

[10] Davis, Natalie Zemon, *A Life of Learning* (New York: American Council of Learned Societies Occasional Paper, No. 39, 1997).

[11] Interestingly, both Miri Rubin and Eva Österberg, who delivered the Natalie Zemon Davis Annual Lectures in 2007 and 2008 respectively, focused on emotions in pre-modern history: Rubin, Miri, *Emotion and Devotion: The Meaning of Mary in Medieval Religious Cultures* (Budapest: Central European University Press, 2009); Österberg, Eva, *Friendship and Love, Ethics and Politics: Studies in Mediaeval and Early Modern History* (Budapest: Central European University Press, 2010).

[12] See, among others, Meyer-Sickendiek, Burckhard, *Affektpoetik: eine Kulturgeschichte literarischer Emotionen* (Würzburg: Königshausen & Neumann, 2005); Kolesch, Doris, *Theater der Emotionen: Ästhetik und Politik zur Zeit Ludwigs XIV.* (Frankfurt: Campus, 2006); Gouk, Penelope and Helen Hills, eds., *Representing Emotions: New Connections in the Histories of Art, Music and Medicine* (Aldershot: Ashgate, 2005); Bredekamp, Horst, *Theorie des Bildakts* (Berlin: Suhrkamp, 2010).

[13] Baasner, Frank, *Der Begriff 'sensibilité' im 18. Jahrhundert: Aufstieg und Niedergang eines Ideals* (Heidelberg: Winter, 1988).

[14] Huizinga, Johan, *The Autumn of the Middle Ages*, trans. Rodney J. Payton and Ulrich Mammitzsch (Chicago: University of Chicago Press, 1996).

[15] Elias, Norbert, *The Civilizing Process* (Oxford: Blackwell, 2000).

[16] Rosenwein, Barbara H., ed., *Anger's Past: The Social Uses of an Emotion in the Middle Ages* (Ithaca: Cornell University Press, 1998), esp. Althoff, Gerd, "Ira Regis: Prolegomena to a History of Royal Anger," pp. 59–74, and, as criticism, Dinzelbacher, Peter, *Warum weint der König? Eine Kritik des mediävistischen Panritualismus* (Badenweiler: Bachmann, 2009); Miller, *Humiliation*, pp. 97–98.

222

[17] Davis, *Life of Learning*.

[18] As of 2008, the Max Planck Institute for Human Development in Berlin, Germany, hosts a research centre on the history of emotions in the modern era. For programme and projects see http://www.mpib-berlin.mpg.de/en/research/history-of-emotions

[19] As to the various concepts and their convergence, see Frevert, Ute et al., *Gefühlswissen: Eine lexikalische Spurensuche in der Moderne* (Frankfurt: Campus, 2011); Dixon, Thomas, *From Passions to Emotions: The Creation of a Secular Psychological Category* (Cambridge: Cambridge University Press, 2003).

[20] See, among others, Goleman, Daniel, *Emotional Intelligence: Why it can matter more than IQ* (London: Bloomsbury, 1996); idem, *Working with Emotional Intelligence* (London: Bloomsbury, 1998).

[21] Rieff, Philip, *The Triumph of the Therapeutic: Uses of Faith after Freud* (San Francisco: Harper & Row, 1966); Lasch, Christopher, *The Culture of Narcissism: American life in an age of diminishing expectations* (New York: W.W. Norton, 1979), and, more recently, Illouz, Eva, *Saving the Modern Soul: Therapy, Emotions, and the Culture of Self-Help* (Berkeley: University of California Press, 2008).

[22] Barker-Benfield, *Culture of Sensibility*; Koschorke, Albrecht, "Alphabetisation und Empfindsamkeit," in *Der ganze Mensch*, ed. Hans-Jürgen Schings (Stuttgart: Metzler, 1994), pp. 605–28; Bermingham, Ann, ed., *Sensation and Sensibility: Viewing Gainsborough's Cottage Door* (New Haven: Yale University Press, 2005); Knott, Sarah, *Sensibility and the American Revolution* (Chapel Hill: University of North Carolina Press, 2009).

[23] Damasio, Hanna et al., "The return of Phineas Gage: Clues about the brain from the skull of a famous patient," *Science* 264 (May 1994): pp. 1102–5; Damasio, Antonio, *Descartes' Error: Emotion, Reason, and the Human Brain* (New York: HarperCollins, 2000); for criticism, see Macmillan, Malcolm, *An Odd Kind of Fame: Stories of Phineas Gage* (Cambridge, Mass.: MIT Press, 2000).

[24] Damasio, Antonio, *Looking for Spinoza: Joy, Sorrow, and the Feeling Brain* (Orlando: Harcourt, 2003), pp. 53–80, 140–79; Daum, Irene et al., "Neurobiological Basis of Emotions," in *Emotions as Bio-cultural Processes*, eds. Birgitt Röttger-Rössler and Hans J. Markowitsch (New York: Springer, 2009), pp. 111–38; as to emotions in decision-making, see Gigerenzer, Gerd, *Gut feelings: The Intelligence of the Unconscious* (New York: Penguin, 2007).

[25] Reisberg, Daniel and Paula Hertel, eds., *Memory and Emotion* (New York: Oxford University Press, 2004), esp. pp. 76–154, 347–89.

[26] Solomon, Robert C., ed., *What is an Emotion? Classic and Contemporary Readings*, 2nd ed. (New York: Oxford University Press, 2003).

[27] Scherer, Klaus R. and Paul Ekman, eds., *Approaches to Emotions: A Book of Readings* (Hillsdale, NJ: Lawrence Erlbaum, 1984); Ekman, Paul and Richard Davidson, eds., *The Nature of Emotion: Fundamental Questions* (Oxford: Oxford University Press, 1994).

[28] Jensen, Uffa and Daniel Morat, eds., *Rationalisierungen des Gefühls: Zum Verhältnis von Wissenschaft und Emotionen 1880–1930* (Munich: Fink, 2008), esp. pp. 35–59 (Jakob Tanner), 101–17 (Daniel Morat).

[29] Elias, *Civilizing Process*, quotes pp. 367, 400.

[30] Plessner, Helmuth, *Limits of Community: A Critique of Social Radicalism* (1924), trans. Andrew Wallace (Amherst, NY: Humanity Books, 1999).

[31] Elias, *Civilizing Process*, p. 441. Interestingly, the postscript to this book did not mention the experience of National Socialism. It is discussed, though, in the chapter "The Breakdown of Civilization" (written in 1961–62) in Elias, Norbert, *The Germans: Power Struggles and the Development of Habitus in the Nineteenth and Twentieth Centuries* (New York: Columbia University Press, 1996), ch. 4. See Fulbrook, Mary, ed., *Un-Civilizing Processes? Excess and Transgression in German Society and Culture: Perspectives Debating*

with Norbert Elias (Amsterdam: Rodopi, 2007).

32 Febvre, Lucien, "Sensibility and History: How to Reconstitute the Emotional Life of the Past," in *A New Kind of History*, ed. Peter Burke (New York: Routledge, 1973), pp. 12–26, quotes p. 26.

33 Febvre, Lucien, *Honneur et Patrie* (Paris: Perrin, 1996), pp. 30–31; Jackson, Julian, *France: The Dark Years, 1940–1944* (Oxford: Oxford University Press, 2001), p. 43; Capdevila, Luc, "The Quest for Masculinity in a Defeated France, 1940–1945," *Contemporary European History* 10, no. 3 (Nov. 2001): pp. 423–45.

34 Febvre, *Honneur*, pp. 31, 54, 67–68.

35 In today's Greek, it means delinquency and negligence (I owe this information to Merih Erol).

36 Crislip, Andrew, "The Sin of Sloth or the Illness of the Demons? The Demon of Acedia in Early Christian Monasticism," *Harvard Theological Review* 98, no. 2 (Apr. 2005): pp. 143–69; Irvine, Ian, "Acedia, Tristitia and Sloth: Early Christian Forerunners to Chronic Ennui," *Humanitas* 12 (Spring 1999): pp. 89–103.

37 Böhme, Hartmut, *Albrecht Dürer, Melencolia I: im Labyrinth der Deutung* (Frankfurt: Fischer, 1991); Schuster, Klaus-Peter, *Melencolia I: Dürers Denkbild*, 2 vols. (Berlin: Gebr. Mann, 1991).

38 Clair, Jean, ed., *Melancholie: Genie und Wahnsinn in der Kunst* (Ostfildern: Hatje Cantz, 2005), French edition: *Mélancolie: Génie et Folie en Occident* (Paris: Gallimard, 2005); Sieber, Andrea and Antje Wittstock, eds., *Melancholie – zwischen Attitüde und Diskurs: Konzepte in Mittelalter und Früher Neuzeit* (Göttingen: V&R unipress, 2009).

39 For decades, this had been the dominant paradigm: Depression was thought to be caused by an unbalancing of three neurotransmitters (serotonin, dopamin, noradrenalin). More recent research has widened the spectrum to include the density of certain brain cells (glia) or the influence of inflammation. Psychoanalysis instead draws attention to unsolved conflicts as the root of depression. For comprehensive information on depression research, see the website of the National Institute of Mental Health:http://www.nimh.nih.gov/health/topics/depression/index.

225

shtml (last access: Nov. 30, 2010).

40 Bailey, Christian, "Honor Bestowed and Felt? Verdienstorden in the Federal Republic after 1945," in *Politische Leidenschaften*, ed. José Brunner (Göttingen: Wallstein, 2010), pp. 61–78; for East Germany that cultivated a particular honour culture, see Speitkamp, Winfried, *Ohrfeige, Duell und Ehrenmord: Eine Geschichte der Ehre* (Stuttgart: Reclam, 2010), pp. 219–21, 240–44.

41 Whitman, James Q., "Enforcing Civility and Respect: Three Societies," *Yale Law Journal* 109, no. 6 (Apr. 2000): pp. 1279–1398.

42 Appiah, Kwame Anthony, *The Honor Code: How Moral Revolutions Happen* (New York: W.W. Norton, 2010), argues that honour is "no decaying vestige of a premodern order" but alive in multiple forms (respect and dignity). He even pushes for a conscious activation of honour "that can drive us to take seriously our responsibilities in a world we share" (p. 179).

43 Social psychologists are (sometimes) the exception to the rule, see Rodriguez Mosquera, Patricia M. et al., "Attack, disapproval, or withdrawal? The role of honour in anger and shame responses to being insulted," *Cognition and Emotion* 22, no. 8 (Dec. 2008): pp. 1471–98.

44 Bourdieu, Pierre, *Outline of a Theory of Practice*, trans. Richard Nice (Cambridge: Cambridge University Press, 1977); idem, *The Logic of Practice*, trans. Richard Nice (Palo Alto, CA: Stanford University Press, 1992).

45 Febvre, *Honneur*, pp. 31, 67.

46 A., "Betrachtung über das Duelliren," *Neue Mannigfaltigkeiten* 1 (1774): p. 765 („im Herzen eingewurzelt").

47 Czernin, Rudolf Graf, *Die Duellfrage* (Vienna: K. Gerolds Sohn in Komm., 1904), p. 3; James, William, "What is an emotion?" in *What is an emotion*, ed. Solomon, pp. 66–76.

48 Montesquieu, The Spirit of Law, Book III, 6 and 7: http://www.constitution.org/cm/sol_03.htm (last access: Dec. 5, 2010).

49 See Miller, *Humiliation*, pp. 116–24 on honour and shame in Icelandic sagas of the Middle Ages; Schreiner, Klaus and Gerd

Schwerhoff, eds., *Verletzte Ehre: Ehrkonflikte in Gesellschaften des Mittelalters und der frühen Neuzeit* (Cologne: Böhlau, 1995).

50 Simmel, George, *Soziologie: Untersuchungen über die Formen der Vergesellschaftung* (Frankfurt: Suhrkamp, 1992), pp. 599–603.

51 Demeter, Karl, *Das deutsche Offizierkorps in Gesellschaft und Staat 1650–1945* (Frankfurt: Bernard & Graefe, 1965), quote p. 290.

52 These actions were stated in a royal Prussian decree from 1843 [Fleck, Eduard, *Die Verordnungen über die Ehrengerichte im Preußischen Heere und über die Bestrafung der Offiziere wegen Zweikampfs* (Berlin: Verl. der Königlichen Geheimen Ober-Hofbuchdruckerei, 1865), pp. 3–4] and remained basically the same throughout the nineteenth and early twentieth centuries.

53 Bayerisches Hauptstaatsarchiv München, IV, A XIII 3, Fasz. 2.

54 Brentano, Lujo, "Über die Duellfrage," *Mitteilungen der Deutschen Anti-Duell-Liga* 29 (1909), p. 6.

55 Welcker, Carl, "Infamie, Ehre, Ehrenstrafen," in *Das Staats-Lexikon: Encyklopädie der sämmtlichen Staatswissenschaften für alle Stände*, 2nd ed., eds. Rotteck, Carl von and Carl Welcker (Altona: Hammerich, 1845–1848), vol. 7 (1847), p. 393; Jhering, Rudolf von, *Der Kampf um's Recht*, 2nd ed. (Vienna, 1872), p. 98; Fischer, Arnold. *Für oder wider das Duell?* (Rostock: Volckmann, 1896), p. 9.

56 Marx, Karl and Friedrich Engels, *Werke*, vol. 29 (Berlin: Dietz, 1970), pp. 331, 336, 562–63.

57 Lassalle, Ferdinand, *Nachgelassene Briefe und Schriften*, ed. Gustav Mayer, vol. 3 (Stuttgart: DVA, 1922), pp. 127–29; vol. 4 (1924), p. 211.

58 Becker, Bernhard, *Enthüllungen über das tragische Lebensende Ferdinand Lassalle's und seine Beziehung zu Helene von Dönniges* (Nürnberg: Wörlein und Comp. 1892), p. 210–15.

59 Gay, Peter, *The Bourgeois Experience*, vol. III: *The Cultivation of Hatred* (New York: W.W. Norton, 1993), pp. 9–33; for its premodern history see Billacois, François, *The Duel: Its Rise and Fall in Early Modern France*, trans. Trista Selous (New Haven: Yale

University Press, 1990).

[60] *Wilhelm und Caroline von Humboldt in ihren Briefen*, ed. Anna von Sydow, vol. 4 (Berlin: Mittler, 1910), pp. 543, 545–46.

[61] Freud, Sigmund, *Briefe 1873–1939*, eds. Ernst Freud and Lucie Freud (Frankfurt: Fischer, 1960), p. 128.

[62] Weber, Marianne, *Max Weber. Ein Lebensbild* (Heidelberg: Schneider, 1950), pp. 473–89.

[63] Freeman, Joanne B., *Affairs of Honor: National Politics in the New Republic* (New Haven: Yale University Press, 2001); Wyatt-Brown, Bertram, *Southern Honor: Ethics and Behavior in the Old South* (New York: Oxford University Press, 2007).

[64] *Guardian*, March 27, 1829. http://www.guardian.co.uk/news/1829/mar/28/mainsection.fromthearchive/print (last access Dec. 7, 2010). The case is discussed in Appiah, Honor Code, ch. 1.

[65] Thimm, Carl A., *A Complete Bibliography of Fencing and Duelling* (1896) (reprint, New York: Benjamin Blom, 1968), pp. 457–58, 479–80. The reasons why the duel became obsolete are discussed in Frevert, Ute, "Honour and Middle-Class Culture: The History of the Duel in England and Germany," in *Bourgeois Society in 19th-Century Europe*, eds. Jürgen Kocka and Allan Mitchell (Oxford: Berg, 1993), pp. 207–40. Appiah's explanation—the democratizing of the duel—is too superficial (*Honor Code*, p. 46). Besides, the duel became commonplace in France too, where the custom did not fade. See Nye, Robert A., *Masculinity and Male Codes of Honor in Modern France* (New York: Oxford University Press, 1993); Reddy, William M., *The Invisible Code: Honor and Sentiment in Postrevolutionary France, 1814–1848* (Berkeley: University of California Press, 1997), pp. 237–38.

[66] Schmid, Joseph C., *Über die Duelle* (Landshut: Weber'sche Buchhandlung, 1802), pp. 9, 28.

[67] Lasson, Adolf, *System der Rechtsphilosophie* (Berlin: Guttentag, 1882), p. 547; Frevert, Ute, *Men of Honour: A Social and Cultural History of the Duel*, trans. Anthony Williams (Cambridge: Polity Press, 1995), pp. 136–44.

[68] See his 1897 argument, in *Die Verhandlungen des achten Evangelisch-sozialen Kongresses* (Göttingen: Vandenhoeck & Ruprecht, 1897), pp. 110–11.

[69] Wagner, Adolf, "Meine Duellangelegenheit mit dem Freiherrn von Stumm," *Die Zukunft* 10 (1895): pp. 408–27.

[70] *Wilhelm und Caroline von Humboldt in ihren Briefen*, ed. von Sydow, vol. 4, pp. 545–46.

[71] *Fürst Bismarcks Briefe an seine Braut und Gattin*, ed. Herbert von Bismarck, 2nd ed. (Stuttgart: Cotta, 1906), pp. 328–29.

[72] *Lassalles letzte Tage: Nach den Originalbriefen und Dokumenten des Nachlasses*, ed. Ina Britschgi-Schimmer (Berlin: Juncker, 1925), pp. 269–70, 280–81.

[73] *Encyclopaedia Britannica*, 8th ed. (Edinburgh: Adam & Charles Black, 1853–1860), vol. 10 (1856), p. 456. See Girouard, Mark, *The Return to Camelot: Chivalry and the English Gentleman* (New Haven: Yale University Press, 1981).

[74] Jhering, *Kampf*, pp. 21, 95–96.

[75] *Preußische Jahrbücher* 84 (1896), p. 376.

[76] Mann, Thomas, *The Magic Mountain*, trans. H.T. Lowe-Porter (London: Penguin, 1960), p. 699.

[77] Mann, Katja, *Meine ungeschriebenen Memoiren*, eds. Elisabeth Plessen and Michael Mann (Frankfurt: Fischer, 1983), pp. 12, 76.

[78] The letter of cand.med. Franque (quoting his Heidelberg fellow student) to the rector of the University of Tübingen from 1817 can be found in *Hauptstaatsarchiv* Stuttgart, E 200 Bü 403.

[79] *Wilhelm und Caroline von Humboldt in ihren Briefen*, ed. von Sydow, vol. 4, pp. 545–46.

[80] Frevert, *Men of Honour*, pp. 168–70.

[81] Berger, "Obsolescence," p. 93. This is both acknowledged and severely criticised by Bowman, James. *Honor: A History* (New York: Encounter Books, 2006); as a morally motivated counter-argument, see Appiah, *Honor Code*.

[82] Honneth, Axel, *The Struggle for Recognition: The Moral Grammar of Social Conflicts* (Cambridge: Polity Press, 1995); Burkhart,

Dagmar, *Eine Geschichte der Ehre* (Darmstadt: WBG, 2006), ch. III.
[83] Gambetta, Diego, *The Sicilian Mafia: The Business of Private Protection* (Cambridge: Harvard University Press, 1993); idem, *Codes of the Underworld: How Criminals Communicate* (Princeton: Princeton University Press, 2009); Labov, William, *Language in the Inner City: Studies in the Black English Vernacular* (Oxford: Blackwell, 1972), ch. 8 (Rules for Ritual Insults); Abrahams, Roger D., "Black talking on the streets," in *Explorations in the Ethnography of Speaking*, eds. Richard Bauman and Joel Sherzer (London: Cambridge University Press, 1974), pp. 240–62; Tertilt, Hermann, "Rauhe Rituale: Die Beleidigungsduelle der Turkish Power Boys," in *Kursbuch JugendKultur*, ed. SPoKK (Cologne: Bollmann, 1997), pp. 157–67. I owe these references to Anja Tervooren. See also Wilms, Yvonne, *Ehre, Männlichkeit und Kriminalität* (Münster: LIT, 2009), pp. 87–120; Mertol, Birol, "Männlichkeitskonzepte von Jungen mit türkischem Migrationshintergrund," in *Junge Muslime in Deutschland*, eds. Hans-Jürgen von Wensierski and Claudia Lübcke (Opladen: Budrich, 2007), pp. 173–94.
[84] See the UN Population Fund's 2000 report on The State of World Population, ch. 3 (honor killings): http://www.unfpa.org/swp/2000/english/ch03.html (last access: Jan. 28, 2011); Appiah, *Honor Code*, ch. 4; Wilms, *Ehre*, pp. 69–86; Eck, Clementine van, *Purified by Blood. Honour Killings amongst Turks in the Netherlands* (Amsterdam: Amsterdam University Press, 2003).
[85] Speitkamp, *Ohrfeige*, pp. 270–77, argues that the honour killings taking place in Western immigrant communities are not "imported" but have grown out of a particular social setting pitching immigrant families against mainstream Western culture. Though not altogether wrong, the argument tends to deny the presence and influence of honour concepts and practices in the immigrants' countries of origin. See, e.g., Dundes, Alan et al., "The Strategy of Turkish Boys' Verbal Dueling Rhymes," *Journal of American Folklore* 83, no. 329 (Jul.–Sep. 1970): pp. 325–49. As to the argument that honour killings are "merely" a feature

of general domestic violence (that is endemic to Western, non-Muslim cultures as well), see the counter-argument by Chesler, Phyllis, "Are Honor Killings simply Domestic Violence?," *Middle East Quarterly* 16, no. 2 (Spring 2009): pp. 61–69.

86 http://soccernet.espn.go.com/print?id=373706&type=story; http://soccernet.espn.go.com/print?id=749212&type=story; http://news.bbc.co.uk/sport2/hi/football/world_cup_2006/5169342.stm (last access: Dec.10, 2010).

87 Roper, Lyndal, "Männlichkeit und männliche Ehre," in *Frauengeschichte – Geschlechtergeschichte*, eds. Karin Hausen and Heide Wunder (Frankfurt: Campus, 1992), pp. 154–72; Müller-Wirthmann, Bernhard, "Raufhändel: Gewalt und Ehre im Dorf," in *Kultur der einfachen Leute*, ed. Richard van Dülmen (Munich: Beck, 1983), pp. 79–111.

88 See the case studies in Peristiany, John G., ed., *Honour and Shame: The Values of Mediterranean Society* (London: Weidenfeld & Nicolson, 1966), esp. Pierre Bourdieu's "The Sentiment of honour in Kabyle Society" (pp. 191–241); Gilmore, David, ed., *Honor and Shame and the Unity of the Mediterranean* (Washington: American Anthropological Association, 1987); Peristiany, John G. and Julian Pitt-Rivers, eds., *Honor and Grace in Anthropology* (Cambridge: Cambridge University Press, 1992).

89 Frevert, Ute, *'Mann und Weib, und Weib und Mann': Geschlechter-Differenzen in der Moderne* (Munich: Beck, 1995), pp. 178–218.

90 Grevenitz, Friedrich August Ferdinand, *Unterricht zur Kenntniß der vorzüglichsten Abweichungen der gesetzlichen Vorschriften des Code Napoleon von den in den neuerlich abgetretenen preußischen Provinzen sowohl den deutschen, als polnischen bisher gültig gewesenen* (Leipzig, 1808), pp. 66, 90.

91 Frevert, *Mann und Weib*, pp. 183, 214.

92 Lange, Helene, "Die Duelldebatten im Reichstag," in *Kampfzeiten*, ed. eadem, vol. 2 (Berlin: Herbig, 1928), pp. 92–100.

93 http://www.icrc.org/ihl.nsf/385ec082b509e76c4125673900

231

3e636d/1d1726425f6955aec125641e0038bfd6 (Section III, Art. 46—last access: Nov. 30, 2010).

[94] Rother, Rainer, ed., *Die letzten Tage der Menschheit: Bilder des Ersten Weltkrieges* (Berlin: Ars Nicolai, 1994), pp. 468–71, 474; Horne, John N. and Alan Kramer, *German Atrocities, 1914: A History of Denial* (New Haven: Yale University Press, 2001), ch. 5; Harris, Ruth, "The 'Child of the Barbarian': Rape, Race and Nationalism in France during the First World War," *Past & Present* 141 (Nov. 1993): pp. 170–206; Gullace, Nicoletta F., "Sexual Violence and Family Honor: British Propaganda and International Law during the First World War," *American Historical Review* 102, no. 3 (Jun. 1997): pp. 714–47; Audoin-Rouzeau, Stéphane, *L'enfant de l'ennemi 1914–1918: Viol, avortement, infanticide pendant la Grande Guerre* (Paris: Aubier, 1995).

[95] Bourke, Joanna, *Rape: A History from 1860 to the Present Day* (London: Virago, 2007), ch. 13.

[96] Treitschke, Heinrich von, *Politics*, trans. Blanche Dugdale and Torben de Bille, vol. 2 (New York: Macmillan, 1916), p. 595. As James Joll confirms, Treitschke's ideas were widely shared by contemporary philosophers and politicians all over Europe [*The Origin of the First World War* (London: Longman, 1992), pp. 217–18].

[97] Quotes in Aschmann, Birgit, "Ehre – das verletzte Gefühl als Grund für den Krieg," in *Gefühl und Kalkül: Der Einfluss von Emotionen auf die Politik des 19. und 20. Jahrhunderts*, ed. eadem (Stuttgart: Franz Steiner, 2005), pp. 151–74.

[98] Frevert, Ute, "Honor, Gender, and Power: The Politics of Satisfaction in Pre-War Europe," in *An Improbable War: The Outbreak of World War I and European Political Culture before 1914*, eds. Holger Afflerbach and David Stevenson (New York: Berghahn, 2007), pp. 233–55.

[99] *Mein lieber Marquis! Friedrich der Große, sein Briefwechsel mit Jean-Baptiste d'Argens während des Siebenjährigen Krieges*, ed. Hans Schumann (Zürich: Manesse-Verlag, 1985), p. 240.

[100] Objects I/6 and I/185 in Rother, ed., *Die letzten Tage der Menschheit*, pp. 454, 473. As to Germania and her national significance, see Brandt, Bettina, *Germania und ihre Söhne: Repräsentationen von Nation, Geschlecht und Politik in der Moderne* (Göttingen: Vandenhoeck & Ruprecht, 2010). For the French national allegory Marianne and her historical metamorphosis, see Agulhon, Maurice, *Marianne au combat. L'imagerie et la symbolique républicaines de 1789 à 1880* (Paris: Flammarion, 1979); idem, *Marianne au pouvoir. L'imagerie et la symbolique républicaines de 1880 à 1914* (Paris: Flammarion, 1989); idem, *Les Métamorphoses de Marianne. L'imagerie et la symbolique républicaines de 1914 à nos jours* (Paris: Flammarion, 2001).

[101] See object I/170 in Rother, ed., *Die letzten Tage der Menschheit*, p. 470.

[102] Gullace, Nicoletta F., *"The Blood of our Sons": Men, Women, and the Renegotiation of British Citizenship during the Great War* (New York: Palgrave Macmillan, 2002), pp. 73–97.

[103] *Robert Capa, Retrospektive*, ed. Laure Beaumont-Maillet (Berlin: Nicolai, 2005), p. 213. Virgili, Fabrice, *Shorn Women: Gender and Punishment in Liberation France* (Oxford: Berg, 2002).

[104] Warring, Anette, "Intimate and sexual relations," in *Surviving Hitler and Mussolini*, eds. Robert Gildea et al. (Oxford: Berg, 2006), pp. 88–128; Frommer, Benjamin, "Denouncers and Fraternizers: Gender, Collaboration, and Retribution in Bohemia and Moravia during World War II and after," in *Gender and War in 20th century Eastern Europe*, eds. Nancy M. Wingfield and Maria Bucur (Bloomington: Indiana University Press, 2006), pp. 111–32; Vervenioti, Tassoula, "Left-Wing Women between Politics and Family," in *After the War was Over*, ed. Mark Mazower (Princeton: Princeton University Press, 2000), pp. 105–21.

[105] Sander, Helke and Barbara Johr, eds., *BeFreier und Befreite: Krieg, Vergewaltigungen, Kinder* (Munich: Kunstmann, 1992); Naimark, Norman M., *The Russians in Germany: A History of the Soviet Zone of Occupation, 1945–1949* (Cambridge: Belknap Press

233

of Harvard University Press, 1995), ch. 2.

[106] Woller, Hans, *Gesellschaft und Politik in der amerikanischen Besatzungszone: Die Region Ansbach und Fürth* (Munich: Oldenbourg, 1986), p. 71; Meyer-Lenz, Johanna, ed., *Die Ordnung des Paares ist unbehaglich: Irritationen am und im Geschlechterdiskurs nach 1945* (Hamburg: LIT, 2000), pp. 71–72.

[107] Berger, "Obsolescence," p. 83.

[108] *Fontanes Briefe*, ed. Gotthard Erler, vol. 2 (Berlin: Aufbau-Verlag, 1989), pp. 213, 299, 377–78.

[109] Allen, Beverly, *Rape Warfare: The Hidden Genocide in Bosnia-Herzegovina and Croatia* (Minneapolis: University of Minnesota Press, 1996); Naimark, Norman M., *Fires of Hatred: Ethnic cleansing in 20th-century Europe* (Cambridge: Harvard University Press, 2001), pp. 167–70.

[110] Recently, East European politicians like Poland's Jaroslaw KaczyÐski and Hungary's Viktor Orbán played the national honour card by claiming that their country had been "insulted" (IHT, Jan. 7, 2011, p. 1). Such pathos resonates well with conservative US citizens who, in August 2010, rallied in Washington to "restore honor." For the right-wing Tea Party movement, American honour had been impaired by President Obama's "apologizing for everything we ever did." What was seen as self-humiliation did not fit the sense of national pride shared by many white, middle-class Protestants in "Middle America." Restoring honour for them was above all claiming back the personal and political self-esteem to which they, as citizens of the "greatest country," felt entitled. http://www.washingtonpost.com/wp-dyn/content/article/2010/08/28/AR2010082801106_3.html?sid=ST2010091201877 (last access: Dec. 11, 2010).

[111] Davis, Natalie Zemon, *Fiction in the Archives: Pardon Tales and their Tellers in Sixteenth-century France* (Stanford: Stanford University Press, 1987), pp. 77–84. As to the growing literature on anger in premodern times, see, e.g., Glick, Robert A. and Steven P. Roose, eds., *Rage, Power, and Aggression* (New Haven: Yale

University Press, 1993); Harris, William V., *Restraining Rage: The Ideology of Anger Control in Classical Antiquity* (Cambridge: Harvard University Press, 2001); Rosenwein, ed., *Anger's Past*; Stearns, Carol Z., "'Lord help me walk humbly': Anger and Sadness in England and America, 1570–1750," in *Emotion and Social Change*, eds. eadem and Peter N. Stearns (New York: Holmes & Meier, 1988), pp. 39–68. Generally, the authors pay little to no attention to gender.

[112] Zedler, Johann Heinrich, ed., *Grosses vollständiges Universal Lexicon Aller Wissenschafften und Künste* (Leipzig/Halle: Zedler, 1732–1750), vol. 63 (1750), col. 501.

[113] Izard, Carroll E., *The Psychology of Emotions* (New York: Plenum Press, 1991), p. 243: "Anger mobilizes energy for action, induces a sense of vigor and self-confidence, and thereby makes individuals more capable of defending themselves."

[114] *Allgemeine deutsche Real-Encyklopädie für die gebildeten Stände [Brockhaus]*, 7th ed. (Leipzig: Brockhaus, 1827), vol. 12, p. 548.

[115] Schlegel, Friedrich, *Theorie der Weiblichkeit*, ed. Winfried Menninghaus (Frankfurt: Insel, 1983), p. 127: „Der *höhere* weibliche Charakter ist—zornfähig männlich."

[116] Ibid., p. 171.

[117] Kant, Immanuel, *Anthropology from a Pragmatic Point of View*, ed., trans. Robert B. Louden (Cambridge: Cambridge University Press, 2006), p. 205. Krünitz, Johann Georg, ed., *Oekonomische Encyklopädie* (Berlin: Pauli, 1773–1858), vol. 236 (1856), p. 12: defined *Weiblichkeit* (femininity) first as "female nature" (*weibliche Natur*), second as "female weakness and defect"(*weibliche Schwachheit und Fehler*).

[118] Basedow, Johann Bernhard, *Das Elementarwerk*, vol. 2 (Dessau: Crusius, 1774), p. 299; vol. 1, p. 218.

[119] Zedler, ed., *Universal Lexicon*, vol. 63 (1750), col. 507; *Real-Encyklopädie [Brockhaus]*, 7th ed., vol. 12 (1827), p. 548.

[120] Cureau de la Chambre, Marin, *Von den Kennzeichen der Leidenschaften des Menschen*, vol. 2, (Münster: Perrenon, 1789), pp.

180, 250, 280–81, 316.

[121] Zedler, ed., *Universal Lexicon*, vol. 63 (1750), col. 510; *Allgemeine deutsche Real-Encyklopädie für die gebildeten Stände [Brockhaus]*, 11th ed. (Leipzig: Brockhaus, 1864–1868), vol. 15 (1868), p. 775.

[122] Meyer, J[oseph], ed., *Das große Conversations-Lexicon für die gebildeten Stände*, 1st ed. (Hildburghausen: Bibliographisches Institut, 1840–1853), vol. 3 (1842), p. 424; *Allgemeine deutsche Real-Encyklopädie für die gebildeten Stände [Brockhaus]*, 10th ed. (Leipzig: Brockhaus, 1851–1855), vol. 1 (1851), p. 630 distinguishes passive anger (*Ärger*) and active rage (*Zorn*). In 1836, H.A. Pierer's Universal-Lexikon attributed rage to "robust" people "with strong will," while anger appertained to "weak and nervous" people (Pierer, Heinrich August, ed., *Universal-Lexikon* (Altenburg: Verlagshandlung Pierer, 1835–1836), vol. 26 (1836), p. 737).

[123] *Real-Encyklopädie [Brockhaus]*, 7th ed., vol. 12 (1827), p. 548.

[124] Ibid., 11th ed., vol. 15 (1868), p. 775; ibid., 10th ed., vol. 1 (1851), p. 630 (stressing the fact that rage by engendering "deeds or words" relieved the soul (*[Gemüt]*).

[125] John Rawls distinguishes "resentment" and "indignation" (as moral reactions to injustice) from "anger" and "annoyance" ("The sense of justice" in idem, *Collected papers*, ed. Samuel Freeman (Cambridge: Harvard University Press, 1999), pp. 96–116, quote p. 111).

[126] See, e.g., *Brockhaus-Enzyklopädie*, 17th ed. (Wiesbaden: F.A. Brockhaus, 1966–1974), vol. 20 (1974), p. 738; ibid., 21st ed. (Leipzig: Brockhaus, 2006), vol. 30, p. 675.

[127] Kring, Ann M., "Gender and Anger," in *Gender and Emotion*, ed. Agneta H. Fischer (Cambridge: Cambridge University Press, 2000), pp. 211–31, quotes pp. 211, 219, 223; Campbell, Anne, *Men, Women and Aggression* (New York: Basic Books, 1993).

[128] Hess, Ursula et al., "Facial Appearance, Gender, and Emotion Expression," *Emotion* 4, no. 4 (Dec. 2004): pp. 378–88, quote p. 378.

[129] Messner, Elisabeth M., "Emotionale Tränen," *Der Ophthalmologe* 106, no. 7 (Jul. 2009): pp. 593–602, esp. p. 601.

[130] Newmark, Catherine, "Weibliches Leiden—männliche Leidenschaft: Zum Geschlecht in älteren Affektenlehren," *Feministische Studien* 26, no. 1 (May 2008): pp. 7–18.

[131] Rousseau, Jean-Jacques, "The Social Contract," in *Social Contract: Essays by Locke, Hume, and Rousseau*, ed. Ernest Barker (London: Oxford University Press, 1978), p. 185; idem, "Emile or on Education," in *The Collected Writings of Rousseau*, eds., trans. Christopher Kelly and Allan Bloom, vol. 13 (Hanover: Dartmouth College Press, 2010), p. 374.

[132] Rousseau, "Emile," Book V.

[133] Laqueur, Thomas, *Making Sex: Body and Gender from the Greeks to Freud* (Cambridge: Harvard University Press, 1990), ch. 5; Honegger, Claudia, *Die Ordnung der Geschlechter: Die Wissenschaften vom Menschen und das Weib* (Frankfurt: Campus, 1991), Virchow's quote p. 210.

[134] Kant, *Anthropology*, pp. 204–05.

[135] Welcker, Carl Theodor, "Geschlechtsverhältnisse," in *Staats-Lexikon oder Encyklopädie der Staatswissenschaften*, eds. Rotteck, Carl von and Carl Welcker (Altona: Hammerich, 1834–1843), vol. 6 (1838), pp. 629–65, quotes pp. 638–41. Welcker heavily relied on Burdach, Carl Friedrich, *Anthropologie für das gebildete Publicum: Der Mensch nach den verschiedenen Seiten seiner Natur* (Stuttgart: Balz, 1837), who served as medical authority on gender differences.

[136] Campe, Joachim Heinrich, *Väterlicher Rath für meine Tochter* (Braunschweig: Verlag der Schulbuchhandlung, 1789), pp. 26, 189–97.

[137] Kant, *Anthropology*, pp. 149–182; Löchel, Rolf, "Frauen sind ängstlich, Männer sollen mutig sein: Geschlechterdifferenz und Emotionen bei Immanuel Kant," *Kant-Studien* 97, no. 1 (Mar. 2006): pp. 50–78.

[138] Kant, *Anthropology*, p. 150. *Allgemeine deutsche Real-Encyclopädie für die gebildeten Stände [Brockhaus]*, 6th ed. (Leipzig: Brockhaus,

1824–1829), vol. 4 (1824), pp. 180–82.

Kant, *Anthropology*, pp. 131–32. In English, *Empfindsamkeit* is translated into "sensitivity," *Empfindelei* into "sentimentality." This conflicts, though, with the translation on p. 209: "She is *sensitive*; he is *sentimental*" ("Sie ist *empfindlich*, Er *empfindsam*").

Darnton, Robert, *The Great Cat Massacre and other episodes in French cultural history* (New York: Random House, 1985), pp. 215–56.

Krünitz, ed., *Encyklopädie*, vol. 75 (1798), pp. 367–80.

Kant, *Anthropology*, p. 209; Herlosssohn, Carl, ed. *Damen Conversations Lexikon* (Leipzig: Volckmar, 1834–1838), vol. 3 (1835), p. 400; vol. 4 (1835), pp. 342–43.

Ibid., vol. 6 (1836), pp. 321–22.

Real-Encyklopädie [Brockhaus], 10th ed., vol. 6 (1852), pp. 322, 681.

Meyers Großes Konversations-Lexikon, 6th ed. (Leipzig: Bibliographisches Institut, 1902–1905), vol. 7 (1904), p. 685.

Brockhaus' Conversations-Lexikon. Allgemeine deutsche Real-Encyklopädie, 13th ed. (Leipzig: Brockhaus, 1882–1887), vol. 7 (1884), p. 649.

Ibid.; *Meyers Konversations-Lexikon*, 5th ed. (Leipzig: Bibliographisches Institut , 1893–1898), vol. 7 (1894), p. 292.

Schlegel, *Theorie der Weiblichkeit*, p. 61.

Trepp, Anne-Charlott, *Sanfte Männlichkeit und selbständige Weiblichkeit: Frauen und Männer im Hamburger Bürgertum zwischen 1770 und 1840* (Göttingen: Vandenhoeck & Ruprecht, 1996), pp. 125–60; Habermas, Rebekka, *Frauen und Männer des Bürgertums: Eine Familiengeschichte (1750–1850)* (Göttingen: Vandenhoeck & Ruprecht, 2000), pp. 315–94.

Staël, Anne Germaine de, *Über Deutschland*, ed. Monika Bosse (Frankfurt: Insel, 1985), pp. 39, 46. Banned by Napoleon in 1810, the book was published in German in 1814.

Welcker, Carl, "Bürgertugend und Bürgersinn," in Rotteck and Welcker, eds. *Staats-Lexikon*, 2nd ed., vol. 2 (1846), pp. 763–

70.

[152] Scheidler, Karl Hermann, "Gemüth," in *Allgemeine Encyclopädie der Wissenschaften und Künste*, eds. Ersch, Johann Samuel and Johann Gottfried Gruber (Leipzig: Brockhaus, 1818–1889), sect. 1, part 57, 1853, pp. 317–18.

[153] Arndt, Ernst Moritz, *Kurzer Katechismus für teutsche Soldaten* (s.l., 1812), pp. 9, 30; idem, *Was bedeutet Landsturm und Landwehr?* (s.l., 1813), p.10. See Frevert, Ute, *A Nation in Barracks: Modern Germany, Military Conscription and Civil Society* (Oxford: Berg, 2004), pp. 22–30; Hagemann, Karen, "Of 'Manly Valor' and 'German Honor': Nation, War, and Masculinity in the Age of the Prussian Uprising against Napoleon," *Central European History* 30, no. 2 (Jun. 1997): pp. 187–220. As to British propaganda, see Colley, Linda, *Britons: Forging the Nation 1707–1837* (New Haven: Yale University Press, 1992), ch. 7.

[154] Welcker, "Geschlechtsverhältnisse," quotes pp. 641, 648–50, 657. As mentioned earlier, though, theories about women's emotionality were diverse and inconsistent. Welcker's colleague Johann Caspar Bluntschli could thus make the opposite argument in 1870: since women were overly "sensitive" and "passionate," they did not fit into politics for which "insight" and "energy" were necessary. Writing after the turbulent 1830s and 1840s, Bluntschli obviously held different opinions both on women and of politics (Bluntschli, Johann Caspar and Karl Brater, eds., *Deutsches Staats-Wörterbuch* (Stuttgart: Expedition des Staats-Wörterbuchs, 1857–1870), vol. 11 (1870), p. 130).

[155] As to how those rules were voiced in popular encyclopaedias and advice manuals, see, e.g., Ersch and Gruber, eds. *Encyclopädie*, sect. 1, vol. 2 (1819), p. 136; *Real-Encyklopädie [Brockhaus]*, 10th ed., vol. 9 (1853), p. 489; Knigge, Adolph Freiherr von, *Über den Umgang mit Menschen*, ed. Gerd Ueding (Frankfurt: Insel, 1977), p. 45 ("the Knigge" published in 1788 became the archetypical manner book and received numerous editions). See Döcker, Ulrike, *Die Ordnung der bürgerlichen Welt: Verhaltensideale und*

soziale Praktiken im 19. Jahrhundert (Frankfurt: Campus, 1994).

[156] Meyer, ed., *Conversations-Lexicon*, vol. 19 (1851), p. 1457; *Meyers Konversations-Lexikon*, 5th ed., vol. 11 (1896), p. 185.

[157] Geitner, Ursula, "'Die eigentlichen Enragées ihres Geschlechts': Aufklärung, Französische Revolution und Weiblichkeit," in *Grenzgängerinnen*, eds. Helga Grubitzsch et al. (Düsseldorf: Schwann, 1985), pp. 181–220.

[158] Welcker, "Geschlechtsverhältnisse," quotes pp. 649–50, 656. Similar arguments were put forward by left- and right-wing authors, see "Geschlechtsverhältnisse," in Blum, Robert, ed., *Volksthümliches Handbuch der Staatswissenschaften und Politik* (Leipzig: Blum, 1848–1851), vol. 1 (1848), pp. 408–12; Riehl, Wilhelm Heinrich, *Die Familie* (1855), 11th ed. (Stuttgart: Cotta, 1897), esp. pp. 10–11.

[159] Hanslick, Eduard, *Vom Musikalisch-Schönen. Ein Beitrag zur Revision der Ästhetik der Tonkunst* (1854), 4th ed. (Leipzig: Johann Ambrosius Barth, 1874), p. 74.

[160] Kirchhoff, Arthur, ed., *Die Akademische Frau* (Berlin: Steinitz, 1897), quotes pp. 5, 29, 67, 148–49. There were more extreme views equalling women's physiological weakness with intellectual deficiency, as suggested by the neurologist Paul Julius Möbius. In 1900, he published his book *Über den physiologischen Schwachsinn des Weibes* (Halle: Marhold, 1900) of which there were nine editions within eight years.

[161] Venedey, Jacob, *Die Deutschen und die Franzosen nach dem Geist ihrer Sprachen und Sprichwörter* (Heidelberg: Winter, 1842), pp. 29, 99, 102.

[162] Flaubert, Gustave, *Correspondance (1862–1868)* (Paris: Conard, 1929), p. 158 (letter from October 6, 1864); Koppenfels, Martin von, *Immune Erzähler: Flaubert und die Affektpolitik des modernen Romans* (Munich: Fink, 2007).

[163] Kolesch, *Theater*.

[164] Cavallo, Guglielmo and Roger Chartier, eds., *A History of Reading in the West* (Cambridge: Polity Press, 1999),

ch. 12; Langewiesche, Dieter and Klaus Schönhoven, "Arbeiterbibliotheken und Arbeiterlektüre im Wilhelminischen Deutschland," *Archiv für Sozialgeschichte* 16 (1976): pp. 135–204, esp. p. 172; Schön, Erich, "Weibliches Lesen: Romanleserinnen im späten 18. Jahrhundert," in *Untersuchungen zum Roman von Frauen um 1800*, eds. Helga Gallas and Magdalene Heuser (Tübingen: Niemeyer, 1990), pp. 20–40.

[165] Cavallo and Chartier, eds., *History of Reading*, ch. 13; Schlaffer, Hannelore, "Lektüre und Geschlecht," *Neue Züricher Zeitung*, July 31, 2010. http://www.nzz.ch/nachrichten/kultur/literatur_und_kunst/lektuere_und_geschlecht_1.7025813.html (last access: Dec. 19, 2010).

[166]Schittenhelm, Rosemarie, ed., *Von Tag zu Tag: Das Große Mädchenbuch*, 23rd ed. (Stuttgart: Frankch'sche Verlagshandlung, 1961), pp. 13–14, 58, 287, 266–67, 273–74. The book was a bestseller in the 1950s and 1960s and saw 25 editions within ten years.

[167] Wobeser, Wilhelmine Karoline von, *Elisa oder das Weib wie es sein sollte* (1795) (reprint Hildesheim: Olms, 1990); Christ, Sophie, *Taschenbüchlein des guten Tones für die weibliche Jugend* (Mainz: Kirchheim, 1888); Peters, F., *Das junge Mädchen im Verkehre mit der Welt* (Mainz: Kirchheim & Co., 1889); *Anstandsbüchlein für junge Mädchen* (Regensburg: Habbel, 1908); Reznicek, Paula von, *Auferstehung der Dame* (Stuttgart: Dieck, 1928); Beck, Fritz, *Der Gute Ton für meine Tochter: Ein Anstandsbrevier für die junge Dame* (Vienna: Pechan, 1960). My thanks go to Rhea Peters who helped to analyse the relevant literature.

[168] The book was first published in 1870, had 15 editions by 1892 and 230 (!) by 1922.

[169] http://web.archive.org/web/20060716064213/http://www.mediagrill.de/Universum.html (last access: Dec. 20, 2010).

[170] This message was generally conveyed by nineteenth- and twentieth-century juvenile literature: Müller, Helmut, ed., *Üb immer Treu und Redlichkeit: Kinder- und Jugendbücher der Kaiserzeit*

(1871–1918) (Frankfurt: Stadt- und Universitätsbibliothek, 1988); Baumgärtner, Alfred Clemens, ed., *Ansätze historischer Kinder- und Jugendbuchforschung* (Baltmannsweiler: Schneider, 1980). For Britain, see Olsen, Stephanie, "Towards the Modern Man: Edwardian Boyhood in the Juvenile Periodical Press," in *Childhood in Edwardian Fiction*, eds. Adrienne Gavin and Andrew Humphries (New York: Palgrave Macmillan, 2009), pp. 159–76.

[171] Frevert, *Nation in Barracks*, pp. 157–99.

[172] Reulecke, Jürgen, *"Ich möchte einer werden so wie die..."* *Männerbünde im 20. Jahrhundert* (Frankfurt: Campus, 2001).

[173] Hitler, Adolf, *Mein Kampf* (Munich: Eher, 1933), p. 392.

[174] http://www.nationalsozialismus.de/dokumente/texte/heinrich-himmler-posener-rede-vom-04-10-1943-volltext.html (last access: Dec. 20, 2010).

[175] http://fr.wikipedia.org/wiki/Émeute (last access: Dec. 20, 2010). In 1835, Pierer's Universal-Lexikon likewise defined *Emotion* as "revolt" (vol. 7, p. 21).

[176] Quote from *Times*, November 13, 1922, in Cowles, Virginia, *Winston Churchill: The Era and the Man* (London: Hamilton, 1953), p. 242 (I owe this reference to Kerstin Singer). As to the emotional charge of election campaigns, see, for Britain, O'Gorman, Frank, "Campaign Rituals and Ceremonies. The Social Meaning of Elections in England 1780–1860," *Past & Present* 135 (May 1992): pp. 79–115; for the US, Bensel, Richard Franklin, *The American Ballot Box in the mid-Nineteenth Century* (Cambridge: Cambridge University Press 2004), pp. 287, 295.

[177] Przyrembel, Alexandra, *"Rassenschande": Reinheitsmythos und Vernichtungslegitimation im Nationalsozialismus* (Göttingen: Vandenhoeck & Ruprecht, 2003), pp. 65–84.

[178] Frevert, Ute, *Women in German History* (Oxford: Berg, 1989), pp. 207–11, 240–47.

[179] *Meyers Großes Konversations-Lexikon*, 6th rev. ed. (Leipzig: Bibliographisches Institut, 1905–1909), vol. 5 (1908), p. 760; *Der Große Herder: Nachschlagewerk für Wissen und Leben*, 4th ed.

242

(Freiburg: Herder,1931–1935), vol. 4 (1932), col. 1327–1328.

[180] Zweig, Stefan, The World of Yesterday. An autobiography (New York: Viking Press, 1945), pp. 73, 78.

[181] *Der Große Brockhaus*, 16th ed. (Wiesbaden: Brockhaus, 1952–1963), vol. 4 (1954), p. 436.

[182] Ibid., vol. 7 (1955), p. 158; *Meyers Lexikon*, 8th ed. (Leipzig: Bibliographisches Institut, 1936–1942) vol. 3 (1937), col. 1290.

[183] Allsop, Kenneth, *The Angry Decade: A Survey of the Cultural Revolt of the Nineteen-fifties* (London: Peter Owen, 1958), p. 9; http://www.britannica.com/EBchecked/topic/25251/Angry-Young-Men; http://www.spiegel.de/spiegel/print/d-41760001. html (last access: Dec. 20, 2010). As to post-war emotional codes in Britain, see Francis, Martin, "Tears, Tantrums, and Bared Teeth: The Emotional Economy of Three Conservative Prime Ministers, 1951–1963," *Journal of British Studies* 41, no. 3 (Jul. 2002): pp. 354–87.

[184] Brody, Leslie R. and Judith A. Hall, "Gender and emotion," in *Handbook of Emotions*, eds. Michael Lewis and Jeanette M. Haviland (New York: Guilford Press, 1993), pp. 447–61; Timmers, Monique et al., "Ability versus vulnerability: Beliefs about men's and women's emotional behaviour," *Cognition and Emotion* 17, no. 1 (Jan. 2003): pp. 41–63.

[185]Hochschild, Arlie R., "Emotion Work, Feeling Rules and Social Structure," *American Journal of Sociology* 85, no. 3 (Nov. 1979): pp. 551–75; eadem, *The Managed Heart: Commercialization of Human Feeling* (Berkeley: University of California Press, 1983); Grandey, Alicia A., "Emotion regulation in the workplace: A new way to conceptualize emotional labor," *Journal of Occupational Health Psychology* 5, no. 1 (Jan. 2000): pp. 95–110.

[186] Schlegel, *Theorie der Weiblichkeit*, p. 99; Reddy, William M., *The Navigation of Feeling: A Framework for the History of Emotions* (Cambridge: Cambridge University Press, 2001), pp. 199–232; Dohm, Hedwig, *Die wissenschaftliche Emancipation der Frau* (Berlin: Wedekind & Schwieger, 1874); Frevert, *Women*, pp. 71–82, 113–30.

243

187 Mergel, Thomas, *Propaganda nach Hitler: Eine Kulturgeschichte des Wahlkampfs in der Bundesrepublik 1949–1990* (Göttingen: Wallstein, 2010); Connelly, Matthew, *A Diplomatic Revolution: Algeria's Fight for Independence and the Origins of the Post-Cold War Era* (New York: Oxford University Press, 2002).

188 See Illouz, *Consuming the Romantic Utopia*; eadem, *Cold Intimacies*.

189 Rieff, *Triumph*; Illouz, *Saving the Modern Soul*.

190 Meyer, ed., *Conversations-Lexicon*, vol. 12 (1848), p. 748; Rein, Wilhelm, ed., *Enzyklopädisches Handbuch der Pädagogik*, 2nd ed. (Langensalza: Beyer 1903–1911), vol. 5 (1906), p. 43.

191 Decety, Jean and William Ickes, eds., *The Social Neuroscience of Empathy* (Cambridge, Mass.: MIT Press, 2009).

192 Trivers, Robert L., "The Evolution of Reciprocal Altruism," *Quarterly Review of Biology* 46, no. 1 (Mar. 1971): pp. 35–57. As to altruism's rise as a moral concept in the nineteenth century, see Dixon, Thomas, *The Invention of Altruism: Making Moral Meanings in Victorian Britain* (Oxford: Oxford University Press, 2008).

193 Ockenfels, Axel et al., "Altruismus, Egoismus, Reziprozität," in *Soziologische Theorie kontrovers*, eds. Gert Albert and Steffen Sigmund (Wiesbaden: VS Verlag, 2011), pp. 119–53; Harbaugh, William T. et al., "Neural Responses to Taxation and Voluntary Giving Reveal Motives for Charitable Donations," *Science* 316, no. 5831 (Jun. 2007): pp. 1622–25.

194 Calhoun, Craig, "A World of Emergencies: Fear, Intervention, and the Limits of Cosmopolitan Order," *Canadian Review of Sociology and Anthropology* 41, no. 4 (Nov. 2004): pp. 373–95; Barnett, Michael, "Humanitarianism Transformed," *Perspectives on Politics* 3, no. 4 (Dec. 2005): pp. 723–40. For a philosophical viewpoint, see Goldie, Peter, "Compassion: A Natural, Moral Emotion," in *Die Moralität der Gefühle*, eds. Sabine A. Döring and Verena Mayer (Berlin: Akademie, 2002), pp. 199–211.

195 See the White House fact sheet on Compassionate Conservatism: http://georgewbush-whitehouse.archives.gov/

244

news/releases/2002/04/20020430.html (last access: Dec. 20, 2010); Berlant, Lauren, ed. *Compassion: The Culture and Politics of an Emotion* (New York: Routledge, 2004), esp. pp. 1–4.

[196] *Documents of German History*, ed. Louis L. Snyder (New Brunswick: Rutgers University Press, 1958), pp. 246–47. (Bismarck's speech of 1881).

[197] Ritter, Joachim and Karlfried Gründer, eds., *Historisches Wörterbuch der Philosophie* (Basel: Schwabe, 1971–2004), vol. 5 (1980), col. 1410–1416; for classical Greek and Roman notions of pity as well as on early Christianity, see Konstan, David, *Pity transformed* (London: Duckworth, 2001).

[198] Müller, Gottfried, "Die Barmherzigkeit Gottes: Zur Entstehungsgeschichte eines koranischen Symbols," *Die Welt des Islams* 28, no. 1/4 (1988): pp. 334–62; Küng, Hans and Josef van Ess, *Christentum und Weltreligionen: Islam*, 7th ed. (Munich: Piper, 2006). My thanks go to Angelika Neuwirth to whom I owe these references.

[199] *Emotional Awareness. Overcoming the Obstacles to Psychological Balance and Compassion: A Conversation between The Dalai Lama and Paul Ekman* (New York: Henry Holt, 2008), ch. 5.

[200] Ritter and Gründer, eds., *Wörterbuch*, vol. 5 (1980), quote col. 1412; Hutcheson, *Essay*, p. 56; Hume, David, *A Treatise of Human Nature*, ed. Ernest C. Mossner (London: Penguin, 1985), pp. 417–18; Rousseau, Jean-Jacques, *Discours sur l'Origine et les Fondements de l'Inégalité parmi les Hommes*, ed. Angèle Kremer-Marietti (Paris: Aubier Montaigne, 1963), p. 84.

[201] Hume, *Treatise*, pp. 367–70; Frazer, Michael K., *The Enlightenment of Sympathy* (Oxford: Oxford University Press, 2010), ch. 2.

[202] Smith, Adam, *The Theory of Moral Sentiments* (Amherst: Prometheus, 2000), pp. 3–30.

[203] dem, *The Wealth of Nations*, ed. Andrew Skinner (Harmondsworth: Penguin, 1973), p. 119.

[204] Ibid., p. 117.

[205] Smith, *Theory of Moral Sentiments*, p. 13. As to other ideas on how to solve the "celebrated Adam Smith Problem," see Hirschman, Albert O., *The Passions and the Interests: Political Arguments for Capitalism before its Triumph* (Princeton: Princeton University Press, 1977), pp. 109–13; Dwyer, John, "Ethics and Economics: Bridging Adam Smith's Theory of Moral Sentiments and Wealth of Nations," *Journal of British Studies* 44, no. 4 (Oct. 2005): pp. 662–87.

[206] Rousseau, *Discours*, pp. 84–87.

[207] Quotes in Schieder, Wolfgang, "Brüderlichkeit," in *Geschichtliche Grundbegriffe*, eds. Otto Brunner et al., vol. 1 (Stuttgart: Klett-Cotta, 1972), pp. 552–81.

[208] Schiller, Friedrich, "Was heißt und zu welchem Ende studiert man Universalgeschichte?," (1789) in *Schillers Werke*, ed. Joachim Müller, vol. 3 (Berlin: Aufbau, 1967), pp. 273–95, quotes pp. 283–84.

[209] Hunt, Lynn, *The Family Romance of the French Revolution* (Berkeley: University of California Press, 1992), ch. 3.

[210] Schieder, "Brüderlichkeit," pp. 565–67.

[211] Hunt, Lynn, *Inventing Human Rights: A History* (New York: W.W. Norton, 2007).

[212] Brown, Christopher L., *Moral Capital: Foundations of British Abolitionism* (Chapel Hill: University of North Carolina Press, 2006); Carey, Brycchan, *British Abolitionism and the Rhetoric of Sensibility: Writing, Sentiment, and Slavery, 1760–1807* (New York: Palgrave Macmillan, 2005); Drescher, Seymour, *The Mighty Experiment: Free Labor versus Slavery in British Emancipation* (New York: Oxford University Press, 2002); Davis, David B., *Inhuman Bondage: The Rise and Fall of Slavery in the New World* (New York: Oxford University Press, 2006).

[213] As to the "sensualist" turn of the eighteenth century, see Williams, Elizabeth, *The Philosophical and the Moral: Anthropology, Physiology, and Philosophical Medicine in France, 1750–1850* (Cambridge: Cambridge University Press, 1994); Vila, Anne,

Enlightenment and Pathology: Sensibility in the Literature and Medicine in 18ᵗʰ century France (Baltimore: Johns Hopkins University Press, 1998); Barker-Benfield, *Culture of Sensibility*, ch. 1.

[214] Koschorke, Albrecht, *Körperströme und Schriftverkehr: Mediologie des 18. Jahrhunderts* (Munich: Fink, 1999), pp. 64–82.

[215] Kant, *Anthropology*, p. 132. This kind of contemporary criticism is echoed by Mullan, John, *Sentiment and Sociability: The Language of Feeling in the Eighteenth Century* (Oxford: Oxford University Press, 1988).

[216] Mackenzie, Henry, *The Man of Feeling* (1771), ed. Brian Vickers (Oxford: Oxford University Press, 2001); Ellis, Markman, *The Politics of Sensibility: Race, Gender and Commerce in the Sentimental Novel* (Cambridge: Cambridge University Press, 2004). As early as 1985, Thomas L. Haskell discussed this as a "real change in sensibility," "associated with the rise of capitalism" (idem, "Capitalism and the Origins of the Humanitarian Sensibility," *American Historical Review* 90, no. 2/3 (Apr./Jun. 1985): pp. 339–61, 547–66).

[217] http://www.spartacus.schoolnet.co.uk/REhoward.htm (last access: Jan.1, 2011); Howard, Derek Lionel, *John Howard: Prison Reformer* (New York: Archer House, 1963); see Foucault, Michel, *Discipline and Punish: The Birth of the Prison* (Harmondsworth: Penguin, 1977), for a critical view.

[218] Prochaska, Frank K., *Women and Philanthropy in Nineteenth-Century England* (Oxford: Clarendon Press, 1980), ch. 5; Summers, Anne, *Angels and Citizens: British Women as Military Nurses, 1854–1914* (London: Routledge, 1988), ch. 1; Himmelfarb, Gertrude, *Poverty and Compassion: The Moral Imagination of the Late Victorians* (New York: Knopf, 1991).

[219] Zedler, ed., *Universal Lexicon*, vol. 41 (1744), col. 744.

[220] Diderot, Denis and Jean le Rond d'Alembert, eds., *Encyclopédie, ou dictionnaire raisonné des sciences, des arts, et des metiers* (Paris: Briasson, 1751–1765), vol. 15 (1765), p. 736.

[221] Larousse, Pierre, ed., *Grand dictionnaire universel du XIXe siècle*

(Paris: Administration du Grand Dictionnaire Universel, 1866–1876), vol. 14 (1875), p. 1316.

222 *Allgemeine deutsche Real-Encyklopädie für die gebildeten Stände [Brockhaus]*, 9th ed. (Leipzig: Brockhaus, 1843–1848), vol. 14 (1847), p. 48.

223 Zedler, ed., *Universal Lexicon*, vol. 21 (1739), col. 552.

224 *Der große Brockhaus: Handbuch des Wissens*, 15th ed. (Leipzig: Brockhaus, 1928–1935), vol. 12 (1932), p. 618; *Brockhaus*, 21st ed., vol. 18 (2006), p. 560.

225 Chismar, Douglas, "Empathy and sympathy: The important difference," *Journal of Value Inquiry* 22, no. 4 (1988): pp. 257–66; Olinick, Stanley L., "A Critique of Empathy and Sympathy," in *Empathy*, eds. Joseph Lichtenberg et al., vol. 1 (Hillsdale, NY: Analytic Press, 1984), pp. 137–66.

226 Lipps, Theodor, *Leitfaden der Psychologie* (Leipzig: Engelmann, 1903); idem, "Das Wissen von fremden Ichen," *Psychologische Untersuchungen* 1 (1907): pp. 694–722; Ritter and Gründer, eds., *Wörterbuch*, vol. 2 (1972), col. 396–99; Chismar, "Empathy," pp. 257–59; Curtis, Robin and Gertrud Koch, eds., *Einfühlung: Zu Geschichte und Gegenwart eines ästhetischen Konzepts* (Munich: Fink, 2009).

227 Vignemont, Frederique de and Tania Singer, "The Empathic Brain: how, when and why," *Trends in Cognitive Sciences* 10, no. 10 (Oct. 2006): pp. 435–41.

228 Schopenhauer, Arthur, "Preisschrift über die Grundlage der Moral," in idem, *Die beiden Grundprobleme der Ethik* (Zürich: Diogenes, 1977), pp. 248–49, 269, 283. As to the concomitant rise of altruism in Victorian Britain, see Dixon, *Invention of Altruism*; for compassion turning into a secular religion of "humanism" in Victorian Britain, see Himmelfarb, *Poverty*.

229 Schopenhauer, "Preisschrift," p. 274.

230 Nietzsche, Friedrich, "Jenseits von Gut und Böse," § 202, 222, 293 in idem, *Sämtliche Werke: Kritische Studienausgabe*, eds. Giorgio Colli and Mazzino Montinari (Munich: dtv/de Gruyter,

1988), vol. 5, pp. 124–26, 156, 236); "Die fröhliche Wissenschaft" § 271, 274, 338, ibid., vol. 3, pp. 519, 565–68.
[231] Nietzsche, Friedrich, "Menschliches, Allzumenschliches," § 50, ibid., vol. 2, pp. 70–71; "Also sprach Zarathustra," ibid., vol. 4, pp. 113–16.
[232] Nietzsche, "Zarathustra," ibid., vol. 4, pp. 77–79, quote p. 78.
[233] Mendelssohn, Moses, "Sendschreiben an den Herrn Magister Lessing in Leipzig," (1756), in Jean-Jacques Rousseau, *Abhandlung von dem Ursprung der Ungleichheit unter den Menschen*, ed. Ursula Goldenbaum (Weimar: Böhlaus Nachfolger, 2000), pp. 235–50, quote p. 239; Meyer-Kalkus, Reinhart, "Apotheose und Kritik des Mitleids: Lessing und Mendelssohn," *Berliner Debatte Initial* 17, no. 1–2 (2006): pp. 36–49.
[234] Hume, *Treatise*, p. 369; Schings, Hans-Jürgen, *Der mitleidigste Mensch ist der beste Mensch: Poetik des Mitleids von Lessing bis Büchner* (Munich: Beck, 1988), ch. III; Diderot and d'Alembert, eds., *Encyclopédie*, vol. 15 (1765), p. 52.
[235] Stocking Jr., George W., *Victorian Anthropology* (New York: Free Press, 1987); Burke, John G., "The Wild Man's Pedigree: Scientific Method and Racial Anthropology," in *The Wild Man Within*, eds. Edward Dudley and Maximillian E. Novak (Pittsburgh: University of Pittsburgh Press, 1973), pp. 259–80; Zimmermann, Andrew, *Anthropology and Antihumanism in Imperial Germany* (Chicago: University of Chicago Press, 2001).
[236] As to the concomitant emergence of sympathy and racism informing the civilising mission of the British Empire, see Rai, Amit S., *Rule of Sympathy: Sentiment, Race, and Power 1750–1850* (New York: Palgrave, 2002); Pernau, Margrit, "An ihren Gefühlen sollt Ihr sie erkennen: Eine Verflechtungsgeschichte des britischen Zivilitätsdiskurses (ca. 1750–1860)," *Geschichte und Gesellschaft* 35, no. 2 (Apr.–Jun. 2009): pp. 249–81.
[237] http://www.nationalsozialismus.de/dokumente/texte/heinrich-himmler-posener-rede-vom-04-10-1943-volltext.html (last access: Dec. 20, 2010).

[238] Krausnick, Helmut, "Judenverfolgung," in *Anatomie des SS-Staates*, eds. Hans Buchheim, Martin Broszat and Hans-Adolf Jacobsen, vol. 2 (Munich: dtv, 1989), quotes pp. 333–34.

[239] Krünitz, ed., *Encyklopädie*, vol. 75 (1798), pp. 348–50.

[240] Whitman, James Q., "What is wrong with inflicting Shame sanctions?," *Yale Law Journal* 107, no. 4 (Jan. 1998): pp. 1055–92, quotes p. 1074 (Thackeray), 1076 (French Code Pénal Progressif, 1832). For German penal practices and legal debates see Evans, Richard J., *Tales from the German Underworld: Crime and Punishment in the Nineteenth Century* (New Haven: Yale University Press, 1998), ch. 2; Foucault, *Discipline*.

[241] Kant, *Anthropology*, pp. 134–35; Krünitz, ed. *Encyklopädie*, vol. 75 (1798), pp. 158–59; Ersch and Gruber, eds. *Encyclopädie*, sect. 1, part 56 (1853), p. 24, talks about the "pleasant feeling" to be free of suffering while sympathising with others' suffering.

[242] Nietzsche, "Jenseits von Gut und Böse," § 225, 222, pp. 160–61, 156.

[243] Sznaider, Natan, *Über das Mitleid im Kapitalismus* (Munich: Bibliothek der Provinz, 2000), pp. 30–33; Orwin, Clifford, "Mitleid: Wie ein Gefühl zu einer Tugend wurde," *Merkur* 63, no. 716 (2009): pp. 1–9.

[244] Koselleck, Reinhart, *Preußen zwischen Reform und Revolution*, 2nd ed. (Stuttgart: Klett, 1975), pp. 641–59, quotes p. 642 (*Großkanzler* Carmer and *Justizrat* Svarez). As to the arguments against capital punishment, see Evans, Richard J., *Rituals of Retribution: Capital Punishment in Germany, 1600–1987* (Oxford: Oxford University Press, 1996); Spierenburg, Pieter, *The Spectacle of Suffering: Executions and the Evolution of Repression* (Cambridge: Cambridge University Press, 1984). As to torture, see Hunt, *Inventing Human Rights*, ch. 2.

[245] Molènes, Alexandre Jacques Denis Gaschon de, *De l'humanité dans les lois criminelles, et de la jurisprudence: sur quelques-unes des questions que ces lois font naître* (Paris: Lacquin, 1830), p. 401: "Renonçons donc à ce supplice que l'humanité réprouve, qui

accoutume la populace à fouler aux pieds la pitié, qui lui apprend comment on brave la honte, et qui lui fait oublier tout sentiment de la dignité de l'homme." See similar comments in Evans, *Tales*, pp. 132–33.

[246] Rousseau, *Discours*, pp. 90, 88 (love as a „fictitious" sentiment „born of social usage").

[247] Smith, *Theory of Moral Sentiments*, pp. 27, 45.

[248] Nietzsche, "Die fröhliche Wissenschaft," § 47, pp. 412–13.

[249] Luhmann, Niklas, *Liebe als Passion* (Frankfurt: Suhrkamp, 1982), p. 9.

[250] Winter, Jay, *Dreams of Peace and Freedom: Utopian Moments in the Twentieth Century* (New Haven: Yale University Press, 2006), ch. 4; Hoffmann, Stefan-Ludwig, ed., *Human Rights in the Twentieth Century* (New York: Cambridge University Press, 2011).

[251] *Meyers Lexikon*, 8th ed., vol. 7 (1939), p. 1455.

[252] Hunt, *Inventing Human Rights*, quote p. 220 (my italics). This confirms the notion of the sacralisation of human life as defended by Joas, Hans, "La dignité humaine: religion de la modernité?," in *L' individu social*, ed. Monique Hirschhorn (Laval: Presses de l'université Laval, 2007), pp. 13–29; idem, "The Emergence of Universalism: An Affirmative Genealogy," in *Frontiers of Sociology*, eds. Peter Hedström and Björn Wittrock (Leiden: Brill, 2009), pp. 15–24.

[253] Calhoun, Craig, "The Imperative to Reduce Suffering: Charity, Progress, and Emergencies in the Field of Humanitarian Action," in *Humanitarianism in Question*, eds. Michael Barnett and Thomas G. Weiss (Ithaca: Cornell University Press, 2008), pp. 73–97; as to post-WWII humanitarianism, see the special issue of Journal of Contemporary History: *Relief in the Aftermath of War*, ed. Jessica Reinisch, vol. 43, no. 3 (Jul. 2008), pp. 371–551.

[254] Sen, Amartya, *The Idea of Justice* (London: Allen Lane, 2009), pp. 403–7.

[255] Rifkin, Jeremy, *The Empathic Civilization: The Race to Global Consciousness in a World in Crisis* (New York: Tarcher, 2009).

251

256 As discussed in Boltanski, Luc, *Distant Suffering: Morality, Media and Politics* (Cambridge: Cambridge University Press, 1999), part III.

257 Berlant, ed., *Compassion*, p. 10; Dean, Carolyn J., *The Fragility of Empathy After the Holocaust* (Ithaca: Cornell University Press, 2004).

258 http://de.wikipedia.org/wiki/Emo (last access: Jan. 30, 2011); Stearns, Peter N., *American Cool: Constructing a Twentieth-Century Emotional Style* (New York: New York University Press, 1994); Geiger, Annette et al., eds., *Coolness: Zur Ästhetik einer kulturellen Strategie und Attitüde* (Bielefeld: Transcript, 2010).

259 Boltanski, *Distant Suffering*, p. xiv.

260 *New York Times*, February 28, 2011 (Articles selected for *Süddeutsche Zeitung*), p. 3.

Index of names

253